A Village at War

Earlston 1914 - 1918

A Village at War

JJ Price

A Village At War

Copyright © 2021 by J J Price. All rights reserved.

This book is sold subject to the condition that it shall not, by way of trade or otherwise, be lent, resold, hired out, or otherwise circulated without the publisher's prior consent in any form of binding or cover other than that in which it is published and without a similar condition including this condition being imposed on the subsequent publisher.

The moral right of Jeffrey Price has been asserted

First published in 2021 by Kindle Direct Publishing

ISBN 9798732118049

Sweet be their sleep now wherever they're lying far
though they be from the hills of their home.

Neil Munro, 'Lament for the Lads'

Contents

Preface ix
Illustrations xiii
Introduction 1
Chapter 1: 1914 7
Chapter 2: 1915 28
Chapter 3: 1915: Achi Baba Nullah 50
Chapter 4: 1916 70
Chapter 5: 1917 87
Chapter 6: 1918 108
Chapter 7: Social Change 142
Chapter 8: The War Memorial 152
Chapter 9: United States of Europe 167
Acknowledgements 171
Endnotes 173
Appendix 1: Roll of Honour 179
Appendix 2: Volunteers 195

Preface

My family came to Earlston in the early 1950s when I was a few months old. Both of my parents served in the RAF in the war, but I cannot remember them discussing their war experiences.

As a child, my only interaction with the village war memorial was on each Remembrance Sunday and as a Cub Scout, marching to the village square and standing to attention in front of the granite column surmounted with a Celtic cross. At the same time, the minister conducted a short service and members of the Royal British Legion lowered and raised their flags. Remembrance Sundays were always the same. In the twelve months between each service, I never thought of reading the names on the memorial, or if I did, I never associated the names on the plaques with families in the village with the same surname.

Many years later, I was researching my family tree when I discovered that my paternal grandfather had served with a Canadian cavalry regiment. He died in 1926, so I never met him, and again, he was never a topic of conversation in our house. But I was intrigued. As I dug further into the record about this man, I found out that he had been born in Wales, qualified as a surveyor, served in the Boer War with the King's Rifle Regiment and then emigrated to Canada.

Who was he?

He was working as a surveyor for the Canadian Pacific Railroad when he decided to enlist. He signed up in a town called Red Deer and joined Lord Strathcona's Horse. I then discovered that, in March 1918, he had taken part in the last ever cavalry charge – 3 squadrons, about 300 men, had charged German positions in a wood just outside the French town of Moreuil.

The Germans had a well-defended position, several machine-gun nests and of course trees, which made it almost impossible to manoeuvre cavalry. But they charged anyway. Canadian sabres against German machine guns! My grandfather was the Squadron Sergeant Major under the command of Lieutenant Flowerdew. During the initial charge, Flowerdew was shot and severely wounded (he died from his wounds the following day). My grandfather was awarded the Distinguished Conduct Medal for his part in the charge. The citation reads:

> For conspicuous gallantry and devotion to duty. In the charge made by his squadron when all the officers had become casualties, he, with admirable coolness and decision, grasped the situation and drew the remainder of the squadron off to the edge of the wood. There he collected and reformed them, and finally cleared the wood completely of the enemy, his judgement and initiative were the means of avoiding many casualties.

The Germans were defeated, and my grandfather survived.

And then my research trail went cold. However, it had whetted my interest in the First World War.

In 2017, the Royal British Legion commissioned a lapel badge to commemorate the one-hundredth anniversary of the Battle of Passchendaele. The pin is poppy-shaped and cast from the brass shell casings recovered from the battlefield. Clay from the area was ground into a powder and mixed with green and red paint used to decorate each poppy.

This tribute seemed to me to capture the struggle for life among the cloying mud and the enemy artillery bombardments. I bought one.

When my pin was delivered, the British Legion had included a card about the *Every Man Remembered* project. The stated aim of this project was that: 'By the end of the centenary in 2018, our objective is to ensure every fallen hero from across the Commonwealth is remembered individually by those living today.'

On the card I received was the name E.W.R. Blake, a second lieutenant in the Somerset Infantry, who died in 1917 and is commemorated at the Menin Gate memorial, in Belgium. I discovered that 2nd Lt Blake had died aged 20 and was the only son (perhaps an only child) of Edward Jarman Blake and Alice Richmond Blake, of The Old House, Crewkerne, Somerset. As it happened, I was going to Ypres, the site of the Menin Gate, in March 2018, to commemorate my grandfather's part in the Battle of Moreuil Wood, so that was my chance to remember 2nd Lt Blake.

The Menin Gate is a massive structure straddling the road from Ypres to Menin. It needs to be massive since it records the names of over 50,000 men who died in battles in the area and but had no remains to bury. It also represents the collective grief of so many nations. The size of the memorial gives us some understanding of the scale of the slaughter.

In the UK an annual Day of Remembrance is held, whereas in Ypres a daily remembrance service is held. Each evening, the main road is closed and buglers from the Fire Department assemble at the memorial and play the 'Last Post' in remembrance and thanks to the fallen. This service has taken place each evening since the end of the war except when Belgium was occupied during the Second World War when the service was moved temporarily to England.

I gave my silent thanks to young Mr Blake, but was left pondering as to how we can remember so many people.

Finding out the few facts about 2nd Lieutenant Blake had whetted my appetite to learn more about this period. However, I began to realize that remembrance of the war dead can be confusing, as they are remembered in various ways.

In Great Britain, people who died on active service, whether killed in action or from wounds or natural causes, were buried in a churchyard of their family's choosing. People who died abroad were buried locally. After the war their bodies were then reinterred in Commonwealth War Graves Commission cemeteries.

Those killed in action, for whom no remains could be found, and those lost at sea, were commemorated on memorials erected by the Commonwealth War Graves Commission.

Alternatively, the war dead were remembered on the war memorials of the towns where they had lived, although some families might have declined this, and could hardly be blamed for holding pacifist views after their loss. Other families might have moved from the village in the intervening years between the death of the family member and the erection of the memorial.

Families could also commemorate the deaths of a family member on a family gravestone in their local churchyard.

Researching my grandfather's exploits was a different project and researching the names of those on the Menin Gate too ambitious, but perhaps gaining some insight into the men named on the village war memorial was achievable. Of course, there would have to be some added context, some form of local history: What was village life like? What was life like for the families of the men at the front? And what was happening nationally and internationally that affected the villagers?

Here then was an opportunity to remember one village's war dead. Every name recorded on the memorial has a story, whether the way the person lived, the way he died or the times he inhabited. By knowing more about these individuals, we shall remember them.

The purpose of this book is to understand something of the life and times of the men named on the Earlston war memorial (see Appendix 1), while acknowledging others where information is available.

Illustrations

1. Hinds, mounted on their heavy horses, with their bondagers.
2. Earlston Rifle Volunteers, 1907.
3. Submarine *U9*'s triumphant return to Wilhelmshaven.
4. Gravestone commemorating Alexander Davidson in Earlston churchyard.
5. James Archibald's grave in Earlston churchyard.
6. John Hewitt, who died during the attack on Aubers Ridge.
7. Soldier wearing a PH or Tube Helmet.
8. German trench barbed wire entanglements.
9. Map of Achi Baba Nullah.
10. The Aikman brothers.
11. Robert and Euphemia Young.
12. Grave of William Wilkie in Earlston churchyard.
13. Family grave in Earlston churchyard commemorating William and Henry Turnbull.
14. Family headstone in Earlston churchyard commemorating James Brockie.
15. Gravestone of John Fraser Young in Earlston churchyard.
16. William Barrie Young's Aero Club Certificate photograph.
17. The gravestone of William Barrie Young in Earlston churchyard.
18. Henry Duff.
19. Family gravestone in Earlston churchyard commemorating Willie Kerr.

20. Volunteer Aid Detachment Registration Card for Barbara MacGregor.
21. Earlston Market Square showing water pump and horse trough erected to commemorate the victory at Battle of Waterloo.
22. Earlston war memorial.
23. Earlston war memorial unveiling ceremony programme.
24. Crowds attending unveiling ceremony.
25. Essex Farm Advanced Dressing Station, photographed in 2018.

Introduction

Earlston lies at the western end of Berwickshire and over the years has flourished mainly because of the fertile soil, which makes for good, productive farming.

The main road from Newcastle to Edinburgh skirts the village, and there used to be a railway branch line connecting mainline routes.

In 1914 the population was about 1,300. The largest single employer was Simpson and Fairbairn, the tweed-weaving company based in the Mid-mill, also known locally as 'New Rhymers Mill'. The mill attracted mill workers from elsewhere in the region.

The village had several shops, including eight grocers, two butchers and bakeries, as well as tailors, drapers and household goods stores.

The other principal employer was agriculture. Most farmworkers relied on annual hiring fairs for employment, with contracts, or 'bonds', typically lasting a year. These workers were hired in pairs – a ploughman, or 'hind', and a female worker, the 'bondager' (Figure 1). Ian MacDougall, in his book *Bondagers,* defines 'bondager' as a term that was applied for over a century, until the eve of the Second World War, to regularly (not merely seasonally) employed, full-time, female farm outworkers, or field workers, in the south-east of Scotland. These women, some only girls, were *bonded* or hired (the younger ones usually with their father or brothers) by farmers, who employed them for a whole range of tasks in and around the farm.

Figure 1. Hinds, mounted on their heavy horses, with their bondagers. Note the bondagers' distinctive dress. (Public domain)

The hind and his bondager were entitled to a tied house or farm cottage. During the First World War, a hind who volunteered, or was conscripted, for military service knew that his family would lose their home and the bondager her job. This consequence would have a significant effect on military recruitment among farmworkers.

At the Earlston Hiring Fair, held in February in 1914, hinds were offered 19 shillings per week plus 1,600 yards of potatoes. Bondagers were offered 12 shillings per week which, in some cases, would rise to 20 shillings during harvest time, plus the offer of a month's food. Boys were hired at between 9 and 13 shillings depending on age and ability.

A farmworker's job was not a well-paid one.

Health care had to be paid for and may have been too expensive for the average worker. Infant mortality was high compared with modern-day rates. From the Government censuses conducted every ten years, two entries relate to child mortality: the number of children born alive and the number of children still living. This data gave the

Government an indication of the levels of obstetric and paediatric care. One mother in the 1911 census had delivered ten live children, of which only five lived.

But for all the poverty, village social life was vibrant. Two local papers, the *Berwickshire News and General Advertiser* and the *Southern Reporter*, have much the same articles as their modern-day equivalents: births, marriages and deaths sections are covered; there is a section on recipes, although the recipes are less exotic and international by modern standards (and no celebrity chefs); and the columns are interspersed with adverts making questionable claims, which would not meet today's advertising standards.

There are the usual seasonal warnings covering a multitude of hazards. For example, in one winter edition, the *Southern Reporter* advised its readers:

> Tobogganing – A boy having had his leg broken in the pursuit of the sport of sledging or tobogganing as was reported in last week's 'Southern' and several accidents having happened since, fortunately of less severity, the sport is to be discontinued out of consideration for the safety of adventurous youth, to whom doubtless the rapid rush down the snowy steep of the White Hill brings a fearful joy.[1]

Interestingly there were no letters complaining that such measures were turning the country into a Nanny State, which might be related to the cost and quality of medical treatment. And if the incapacitated youth was a wage-earner (school-leaving age was 12 years), there could be additional financial hardship due to the loss of income.

Some of the clubs and societies still exist, whereas others have fallen by the wayside. The bowling club still meets, and the curling club has been resurrected, meeting at a nearby indoor rink rather than the outdoor rinks of the early 1890s. The rugby club still survives, as does the golf club, albeit without a course.

The village boasted an orchestra, which was a feature of musical evenings and operatic shows. The school plays and operettas involved a substantial number of villagers, in addition to the school staff and pupils; for example, a newspaper review of the production of *The Magic Ruby* notes that Archibald Black, a railway signalman, built the scenery, and Samuel Fisher, who ran the village house painting and decorating business, was in charge of the artwork.

Another feature of society at the time was the strict class system. Such was the master–servant mindset that the Royal Flying Corps nominated the gunner–observer in the rear seat of the aircraft as the 'captain' and the pilot was the 'driver', which derived from the master–chauffeur model. It may have worked well when being driven around in one's Rolls Royce, but was doomed to failure in aerial combat. Fortunately, the Royal Flying Corps (RFC) saw the error of its ways and changed to the system where the captain and the pilot were the same person. There are other examples of the class system at work. The Earlston war memorial lists the names of three officers. Two officers, both captains, were from middle-class families, one the son of a bank manager and the other the son of the village doctor. Senior officers in the British military were almost exclusively the sons of the landed gentry, as in the case of the third officer, a brigadier general, who was the eldest son of the Earl of Haddington. Casualties reported in battalion War Diaries also reflected the class structure. Officers who were casualties are listed by name and rank, whereas 'Other Ranks' are simply reported as numbers killed or wounded.

Nonetheless, a strong sense of community prevailed. To some, the actions of villagers could be seen as nosiness, but generally, their intentions were good. One example, recalled by Willie Alchin, a village baker – in his book *As I recall: Childhood Memories of Newstead* – related an act of neighbourliness:

Dr Young, the village doctor, was in the habit of having his suits made by a local tailor named Adam Mather, who conducted a small business in Earlston and was one of the worthies of his day.

On one occasion when the doctor was ordering a suit, he told Adam, 'Now Adam, I don't want you to make the waist of the trousers so high this time'.

To which Adam replied: 'Noo look here doctor if ye dinna ken what's wrang wi ye, aa the folk in Earlston ken what's wrang wi ye, ye have trouble wi yer kidneys and ye hae tae keep them warm and ah'm gang tae see ye keep them warm, and if yo like it or no, ah'm making yer breeks the same as ah've aye made them and that's the end o'it.'[2]

At the beginning of the twentieth century, Great Britain was engaged in the Second Boer War.

On the last Friday of January 1900, Earlston volunteers left to serve in South Africa. At Earlston railway station, which was decorated with flags, the men were given an enthusiastic send-off by well-wishers as a pipe band played.

When the war ended in 1902, two returning soldiers, Robert Young and James Maltman, were given an equally enthusiastic welcome. School children were released from their classes to greet the returning heroes at the train station, and workers at the tweed mill were given an hour off work to join in the welcome.

Robert Young and another survivor of the South-African war, Stewart Paterson, would serve again in 1914, but they would not live to enjoy another such welcome.

Although war was still in recent memory, villagers must have been given some hope when, on 20 May 1910, the funeral of King Edward VII took place in London. The funeral was the largest gathering of European Royalty, with the kings of Prussia, Greece,

Spain, Norway, Denmark, Portugal and Bulgaria in attendance. All told, seventy states were represented, so it would have been natural to assume that such a gathering would secure a continuing peace in Europe. The last European war between Germany and France had ended in 1871. But the peace and calm were illusionary.

On 28 June 1914, the Arch Duke France Ferdinand was assassinated in Sarajevo, and with his death, European nations sided with one another to settle old scores. One such score was the Franco–Prussian War, which Germany felt was unresolved. When Germany declared war on France it was apparent that it would need to enter Belgium first. In signing the Treaty of London in 1839, Great Britain had pledged to defend Belgium in the event of an invasion. Perhaps thinking that this was a bluff, Germany invaded Belgium in August 1914. Great Britain immediately declared war on Germany and began the mobilization of its military. And so began the First World War.

It is difficult to comprehend the effect of this on the lives of ordinary British people. At the outset, the sense of fair play meant that people firmly believed that defending Belgium was the right thing to do. Britain had a vast empire spanning a quarter of the globe, and therefore there must have been a feeling that Britain was invincible. But Britain was ill-prepared and, since this was the first conflict using 'industrial warfare' tactics, casualty rates would be unprecedented.

Chapter 1

1914

The first to answer the call was Adam Girdwood, but others would follow. Adam was in the Royal Navy Reserve and had been called up by the general mobilization order issued by the Government on Saturday, 1 August 1914.

Adam was born and raised in Earlston. As a young man, he had joined the Royal Navy and served onboard HMS *Perseus*, patrolling the Persian Gulf to suppress gun-running. When he left the service the previous Christmas, he had taken a job with the Post Office in Selkirk. He was called back for a month in February to take part in the Fleet Review at the Spithead, as a crew member of HMS *Hogue*. When he got the summons to mobilize, he cycled the 12 miles from Selkirk to Earlston to say goodbye to his mother, Agnes, and his sister Jane. Then he made his way to the railway station, where he caught the 05.20 train that took him to the Royal Navy dockyard in Chatham.

When Robert Burns left school, he did not follow his father, William, to become a joiner. Instead, Robert became an apprentice watchmaker. In 1906, perhaps looking for excitement and adventure, Robert enlisted in the 16th Lancers. When he left the army, became a reservist, and he too caught the train that would take him to the Corps of Lancers headquarters and the biggest adventure of his life.

George Graham was an Earlston postman and a reservist in the Gordon Highlanders. His journey started at the station for the first of many trains that would take him to Aberdeen and the Gordons' headquarters.

Albert Wood was another postman and a reservist with the Army Medical Corps. Albert was on holiday when his mobilization order came through, so it was sitting on the doormat waiting for his return.

William Lountain was a reservist with the Royal Artillery. He too made his way to the station and onwards to the Royal Artillery headquarters.

Two brothers, William and Alexander Milne, were army regulars. William was a Sergeant Major in the Royal Artillery and his younger brother, Alexander, was a lance sergeant in the 1st King's Own Scottish Borderers (KOSB). Alexander was with the Battalion in Lucknow, India, and was already making preparations to return to Britain when the mobilization order came through.

The last two reservists left Earlston on Thursday, 6 August. Charles Edward and William Thomson were given 'a very hearty send-off by a sympathetic company of spectators'.[3] This farewell was in contrast to the departure of the Territorial Forces.

In 1863, Captain Mitchell, a veteran of the Crimean War, raised the Earlston Rifle Volunteers. By 1887, they had transferred to the King's Own Scottish Borderers forming the 2nd Volunteer Battalion, commanded by Colonel Hope of Cowdenknowes.

In 1908, the Volunteers battalions merged with other militia and yeomanry companies to form the Territorial Force. Earlston men formed D Company 4th Battalion, King's Own Scottish Borders (Figure 2).

A Village at War

Figure 2. Earlston Rifle Volunteers, 1907. The Volunteers eventually became D Company, 4th Battalion King's Own Scottish Borderers.

On Monday, 3 August, a general mobilization order was issued for army personnel and the territorial forces. The following evening, men from the Earlston Territorials met to plan their mobilization. On Wednesday, the men gathered in the Market Square for rifle and kit inspection. They mustered again that evening. Over these few days and nights, the Market Square filled with men in khaki as the reservists made their way to the station and the Territorials gathered for their evening inspections. Naturally, civilian friends of the soldiers also congregated in the square to discuss the news and rumours, then speculate on what might lie ahead. Weatherston's, the jeweller, and Rutherford's, the barber and tobacconist, were popular meeting places.

On Thursday morning, the men mustered for a final inspection. Twenty Territorials had arrived from nearby Lauder, and together the men marched to 4th Battalion King's Own Scottish Borderers (KOSB) headquarters in Galashiels, some 8 miles away.

Their departure was muted and in contrast with the send-off troops bound for the South-African war had been given years earlier. At 06.30 the order was given to, 'Form fours. Quick march.' The sun was shining with a clear blue sky for the first step of their journey. Of the thirty Earlston men marching along the High Street that morning five would not return. The village would lose almost ten times that many. A local newspaper reported that, as if by premonition, 'Not a single cheer or demonstration of any kind greeted the departing troops'.[4]

A fatigue party of Territorials had been sent to collect ammunition from the Black Hill rifle range. Just outside the town, they stopped by the railway tracks to wave goodbye to Charles Edward and William Thomson, the last reservists, as their train made its way south before they joined their comrades for their journey.

When three of the Territorials failed their medicals, John Steedman, the bank manager and local commanding officer of the Territorials, was ordered to find an additional six men 'Willing to return to the Colours', to complete a full battalion number. Twelve men volunteered and six were selected. They left for Galashiels on the Saturday following their comrades' departure.

And with the departure of these men, a way of village life departed, never to return.

By Sunday, 16 August, Lord Binning and Colonel Hope had each received a telegram from the War Secretary, requesting them, 'To use all the influence their power to further this national object'.

Lord Binning, or George Ballie-Hamilton, was the eldest son of the Earl of Haddington. The family residence was Mellerstain House, a few miles from Earlston, and the family owned most of the land in and around the village. The family was, as a consequence, considerably influential. Lord Binning had been His Majesty's Lieutenant of Berwickshire since retiring from the army in 1907, but had remained in the military Territorial Force as Commanding Officer of the Lothians and Border Horse.

Colonel Hope was the last surviving son of the Hon. Charles Hope, MP for Linlithgowshire and Lord Lieutenant of the Isle of Man, the third son of the fourth Earl of Hopetoun. Colonel Hope's mother, Lady Isabella Helen Hope, had inherited the St Mary's Isle Estate, Stewart of Kirkcudbright, from her brother, the Earl of Selkirk.

Colonel Hope was educated at Eton and Sandhurst. He served in the King's Royal Rifle Corps 1863–1883, then on leaving the regular army, joined the 2nd King's Own Scottish Borderers (KOSB) Volunteer Battalion, retiring in 1906 with the rank of Colonel.

Colonel Hope lived at Cowdenknowes, a large country house a mile or so from the village, and closely identified with county and Earlston affairs. He served as Chairman and President of several Earlston committees, including the School Board, the Men's Committee and the War Memorial Committee. He died in 1930.

In response to the War Secretary's request, Lord Binning wrote a letter to the local newspapers

> Sir,
>
> HRH the Prince of Wales having opened a National Relief Fund in this grave crisis of the Empire, I would appeal to the people of Berwickshire to come forward patriotically and support it. My military duties do not permit even one day's absence from my post to attend meetings in the County and make personal appeal but probably this is unnecessary. As will be seen from the advertisement in your columns the Convener of the County and I am making arrangements for the collection of subscriptions in each Parish and Burgh and I have no doubt whatever that every one will respond heartily. Thanking you in anticipation for publishing this letter. I beg to remain.
>
> Your obedient servant,
BINNING,
Lord Lieutenant the County of Berwick[5]

Lord Binning pledged £100 to the fund, Lord Tweedsmuir pledged 100 guineas and Colonel Hope an ostentatious £500.

For his part, Colonel Hope held a public, albeit for men only, meeting in the hall of the Corn Exchange.[6]

Hope sought to allay concerns by saying that the war should not be viewed as a great calamity but that, 'War is over-ruled by Providence, and that, sooner or later, good in some way will come out of it'. He stressed that the war was unprovoked, referring to the Foreign Secretary, Sir Edward Grey, who was also MP for Berwick, and his speech to Parliament. Hope cautioned that the war might be lengthy, but he was convinced that the country would see it through under the leadership of Lord Kitchener, the War Secretary. The mere mention of Kitchener's name provoked loud and sustained cheering from the audience and Hope used this enthusiasm to encourage men to volunteer for Kitchener's New Army. Kitchener was seeking to raise an army of 100,000 men, and Hope looked to the men of Earlston and district to play their part. At the time the British military was against conscription. believing that volunteers made much better soldiers and sailors than pressed men. However, such would be the attrition rate that this policy became unsustainable and conscription was introduced in 1916.

Hope also talked about the contribution that was being made by the 'colonies'. Like many small Scottish towns, Earlston had seen a number of its residents emigrate to seek a better life abroad. Jack Taylor, the son of Andrew Taylor, an Earlston grocer, had emigrated to Australia and he enlisted in Australia Expeditionary Force and was later severely wounded. Frank Kerr had emigrated to Canada and fought in the South-African war with the Canadians before emigrating again, this time to Australia, where he enlisted in the Australian army. Five men from Earlston who had emigrated to Canada and enlisted to fight for King and Empire would not survive.

Following Colonel Hope's speech, a Recruitment Committee was formed to encourage men to volunteer. Because both Hope and John Steedman were Justices of the Peace, they could attest the men and Dr Young was able to conduct the preliminary medical exam. The committee members were drawn from a broad stratum of village society: Colonel Hope, Captain John Steedman, Messrs John Simpson (wool manufacturer), Tom Murdison (plumber), William Kerr (joiner), Sergeant John Burrell, Samuel Fisher (house painter), John Thompson, Robert Herbertson (farmer, Fans), John Leggat (farmer, Legerwood), Robert Martin (Legerwood) Henry Hewat (farmer, Sorrowlessfield) and John MacKay (estate factor). The committee had the power to add to their number.

The declaration of war had other immediate effects on villagers. The Government had taken over the railway system, and all excursion tickets were suspended until further notice. The cheap tickets issued for the August bank-holiday weekend were cancelled, much to the chagrin of those wanting to make the most of the holiday.

The tweed mill, a major employer in the village, was 'closed until further notice'. About 25 per cent of the mill's production had been exported to Germany, so that market vanished. Fortunately, the mill soon reopened after the company won Government contacts to produce blankets and material for uniforms.

Inevitably food prices rose. The *Berwick Advertiser* reported:

> One result of the outbreak of hostilities on the Continent was a great rise in the price of provisions and other commodities, owing to the expected stoppages from abroad. Earlston people, however, did not completely lose their heads as did housewives in some of the larger towns, by making a run upon groceries and stores, and by this means causing the very calamity they were anxious to avoid.

For several years there had been a steady supply of fish from local fishing ports such as Eyemouth. Catches were available on

Tuesdays and Saturdays and, as a consequence, fish and chips became a traditional meal on those days. At the outbreak of war, fishing vessels were reluctant to venture into the North Sea, and so the supply of fish stopped. The *Berwick Advertiser* reported optimistically: 'It is expected, however, that the fish supply will be resumed as soon as the German fleet in the North Sea has been either destroyed, crippled, or bottled up in German waters.'

Petrol was rationed, but few villagers owned cars. However, a company that often put on 'an exhibition of cinema pictures' at the Corn Exchange, had to cancel due to lack of petrol. Farmers relied on horses rather than tractors, but the army started requisitioning horses, which put pressure on farmers and farmworkers. In the longer term, this inevitably hastened the demise of the use of heavy horses on farms. The war would put greater emphasis on food security, thereby demanding greater efficiency – that is, mechanization – in agriculture and less labour-intensive farming techniques. On one day in early August, it was reported that Colonel Hope lost 'four superb specimens' to the army, and Robert Smart, landlord of the Red Lion Hotel, lost three. Other businesses were affected: Ralph Dodds, a grocer, had one horse requisitioned, as did Robert Murdison, plumber, and George Stewart, a local dairyman. Other horses were inspected, but not taken. However, the army would return in its search for suitable animals.

Farmers were hardest hit as heavy horses that were trained to plough could not be replaced overnight. The Government asked for more food to be produced by farmers while, at the same time, taking away the very tools needed to achieve this aim – men and horses. And since the railways had to prioritize the war effort, horse-drawn vehicles were in high demand. Inevitably the price of oats and hay soared, adding to the worries of the farmers. At least family pets were spared when, after pleas from children concerned about the welfare of their ponies, Lord Kitchener issued an order that no horse less than 15 hands should be purchased by the army.

The Government rushed through the Defence of the Realm Act, which gave it broad powers to introduce legislation deemed necessary to win the war. Some of the laws that were introduced seem trivial now. For example: it became illegal to whistle for London cabs lest people thought it was an air-raid warning; and burning bonfires and flying kites were banned, in case these methods were used to communicate with the enemy. Some laws existed until quite recently, such as: licensing laws were changed to ensure pubs closed during the afternoon so that workers could maintain war production; and British Summer Time was introduced and still exists. It became illegal to loiter near bridges, railway lines and other areas of infrastructure, in case these became targets for saboteurs. In response to this last law, the Home Defence was formed, 'to inspect railways, bridges, roads, telegraph lines, signals and railway lines day and night to make sure they had not been tampered with'.

Local clubs and organizations were sensitive to the impact of the war. The Annual Flower Show, scheduled to take place later in August, was cancelled, and Earlston Rugby Club agreed not to schedule any matches beyond Christmas.

However, the annual Boy Scout camp under the leadership of Scout Master Tom Murdison went ahead as planned. Scouts would also be given duties to help with the war effort, such as cyclist messengers, ambulance and signallers. Coloured arm badges were developed to identify the role that had been assigned to the wearer.

Fundraising became a national obsession. Lord Binning had announced the establishment of the Prince of Wales National Relief Fund, but charitable donations were needed in other areas. The Belgium Relief Fund was, unsurprisingly, an early example. The Red Cross needed money for hospital accommodation and practical nursing. This organization also recognized the needs of the families of soldiers and sailors.

In October 1914, Lord Kitchener asked that a 'Smokes for Soldiers and Sailors Fund' be formed. Initially targeted at providing smoking materials to the wounded men in hospitals and convalescent homes, it soon spread to support all service personnel.

Two local newspapers, the *Berwickshire News and Advertiser* and the *Berwickshire Journal*, embraced this initiative and started their own 'Something to Smoke' fund. Readers were asked to donate sixpence, which went directly to buying tobacco products. The newspapers published the names of the donors and the amount they had given. In some cases, donations were made for named individuals, who the donor wanted the tobacco to reach. The newspapers encouraged service personnel to write to the paper offering thanks to those who made donations.

In Earlston, a War Guild was formed to raise money to fund other ways to lift the morale of the service personnel. Socks were knitted, parcels containing 'luxuries' such as shortbread and chocolate were sent to the forces personnel. Schools were also encouraged to raise funds.

In this way, people back home felt that they were able to show support for their men and contribute directly to the war effort. And the funds raised were much needed.

The fundraising efforts of Earlston was led by Mrs Hope of Cowdenknowes, who devoted much of her energy to this cause. She organized an informal meeting of friends at the manse to discuss the matter, which led to calling a meeting of the village womenfolk in the Corn Exchange, 'for the help of the soldiers and sailors engaged in the present war'. The response encouraged about fifty women to attend, and it was agreed that they would organize themselves to provide articles of clothing for military personnel. Mrs Hope was elected as President of the group, and Mrs Clement Hope of Chapel-on-Leader was elected Vice-President. Mrs Young, the doctor's wife, was elected as secretary and Mrs Steedman, the wife of the bank manager, was elected Treasurer. Additionally, a committee was formed of twelve ladies, with fourteen collectors to canvass for funds to buy the material which would be made into garments for the soldiers and sailors.

On 23 September 1914, the nation woke to the catastrophic news that three British cruisers, HMS *Aboukir*, HMS *Cressy* and HMS *Hogue* had been attacked and sunk by the German U-Boat, *U9*. The attack took place off the coast of Belgium and resulted in the deaths of 1,450 sailors. Earlstonians remembered that Adam Girdwood, the Royal Navy reservist, had been a crew member on board HMS *Hogue* during the Spithead Review. Thankfully Adam was then serving on another vessel.

The *U9* returned to a triumphant welcome in Wilhelmshaven and the German Government was quick to capitalize the propaganda value and issued postcards marking the event (see Figure 3). The German High Command was now firmly convinced of the full potential of its submarine fleet and the Royal Navy recognized that it needed to drastically alter its tactics in dealing with the German submarine threat.

Figure 3. Submarine U9's triumphant return to Wilhelmshaven. (Public domain)

Submarine *U9* and its commander, Otto Weddigen, would return to haunt the Royal Navy and make news in Earlston just three weeks later. On 15 October, five British cruisers were on patrol off the Aberdeenshire coast. Since the sinking of the three ships in September, the Royal Navy had developed a tactic of zig-zagging and altering the vessels' speed to make it difficult for submariners to predict the course of the ships and, therefore, to fire torpedoes with any accuracy. However, two cruisers, HMS *Hawke* and HMS *Endymion* stopped in the water to launch a boat to transfer the ship's mail. The vessels were stationary for only a few minutes, but were left behind the rest of the group. When the small boat was recovered, the two ships steamed on a steady course and speed to catch up the flotilla. But *U9*, under the command of Otto Weddigen, was operating in the area and this was just the opportunity he needed. He launched one torpedoed which struck HMS *Hawke*, sinking her within ten minutes. Over 500 men were killed and only 70 rescued. One of those killed was Alexander Davidson, an able-bodied seaman.

Davidson had been an attendant at the College of Art in Edinburgh and a Royal Fleet Reservist. He had heeded the mobilization order and joined his ship on 1 August, the day after his marriage to Margaret Paxton, a domestic servant living and working in Edinburgh. After Davidson had left for the war, Margaret moved to Earlston to be closer to her sister Mary and her husband, Robert Johnston, as well as Margaret's mother, who lived with Mary and Robert.

When Davidson was killed, Margaret received the standard telegram with the message: 'The King commands me to assure you of the true sympathy of His Majesty and the Queen in your sorrow – Winston S. Churchill'.

In the last few weeks of 1914, Margaret developed tuberculosis and died on 2 January 1915. She is buried in Earlston Church cemetery where her headstone bears the inscription: 'In memory of

A.M.S. Davidson who was lost at sea through the sinking of HMS Hawke 15.10.1914. Also his wife Margaret Paxton who died in Earlston 2.1.15' (Figure 4).

Davidson's name does not appear on the Earlston war memorial, but he is remembered on the Chatham Naval Memorial.

Figure 4. Gravestone commemorating Alexander Davidson in Earlston churchyard.

The drive for recruits only exceeded the nation's obsession with fundraising.

The newspapers began to focus relentlessly on recruitment. Most weeks the papers included a 'Roll of Honour', listing the names of every man who had enlisted the previous week from each town, village or parish. Some papers published tables showing the total number of recruits for each district. Farm servants were a particular target of the recruiters. An article appeared in the *Edinburgh Evening News* accusing farmers and farm servants of 'dodging their duty':

> Recruiting In Country Districts:
> Are the Hinds Hanging Back?
>
> A very general feeling prevails upon the Borders (writes a country correspondent) that the young men in the rural districts have so far failed to grasp the seriousness of the present crisis with its urgent call for personal Service. In the towns the response by the workers has been, on the whole, satisfactory: but among the farm servants there has not been, as yet, anything like the same readiness to rally to the clouds. There are parishes – and fairly populous parishes too – from which not a single recruit has gone forth, those who might be supposed to have influence with the young men having been apparently too engrossed with their own personal affairs – buying and selling – to mind the interests and needs of the nation. Farmers, as a class, stand to benefit financially by the war, and this autumn from their sales of draught stock many have cleared largely increased profits.
>
> *Dodging Duty*
>
> While grain was still in the fields, farmers may have had some excuse for keeping hold of their men: but it is weeks ago since it was all safely harvested, and the flow of recruits from the farms has not yet begun, not is there any evidence that employers generally are

troubling themselves about the seeming apathy of the ploughmen. Last week, in various parts of the of the Border district, large numbers of farm work horses were purchased on behalf of the Government. With these many of the sellers parted not ungrudgingly – as much as £100 was paid for a horse at the Hawick parade, and £90 at Jedburgh – and replacement need not necessarily be a difficult matter. At these horse sales the large number of farm servants of suitable physique for soldiering was noted and commented on, and suggested the reflection that farmers might profitably spare a little of their leisure in an endeavour to stimulate their interest in the war, and in opening their eyes to a vision of duty plainly demanded of them.

Farmers Must Help

That the indifference among the hinds – largely due, it is commonly believed, to lack of encouragement by their masters – is causing disappointment in local military quarters, is obvious from the terms of an appeal for recruits for the Lowland Territorial Division, signed by the leading officials of the women's political associations in Roxburghshire – Liberal and Unionist – and at present being circulated in that county. In that appeal – which is signed by, among others, Colonel Sir Richard J. Waldie Griffith – it is stated that 'Roxburghshire has done well, but Roxburghshire, and especially the country districts, can do much better.' If this appeal is to bear fruit, it must be backed up by the practical support of the farmers, whose action at this perilous period in our country's history will be watched with critical interest.[7]

No evidence was offered to support the claims, and the perception persisted even though the reality was very different.

On the last Thursday of October, Colonel Griffith and Captain Mabbot led the reserve battalion of the King's Own Scottish Borderers as they marched into Duns. The men were on a route march that passed through Duns, Lennel, Swinton, Greenlaw, Gordon and Earlston to recruit as many men as possible.

The battalion, including the pipe band, formed up in two sections in front of Duns Town Hall around 6.30 p.m.

Baillie Lamb, the senior Baillie for the Burgh, welcomed the men and apologized on behalf of the Provost, who was indisposed and therefore could not attend in person.

In his address, Baillie Lamb said that he was proud to welcome such a fine body of men and a good regiment. He hoped the march through the county would encourage men of the district to enlist. Lamb expressed his disappointment in not seeing many farm servants in the crowd, as he thought that they were just the class of men to fill the ranks of the army, and concluded the welcome by saying that there was no county better than Berwickshire to supply the right men, and no regiment offered a better record than that of the King's Own Scottish Borderers.

In his reply, Colonel Griffith said that he too would like to see more farm servants come forward. He stated that the people needed not fear an invasion of Scotland, as this was impossible. He then said that farm servants, if they did enlist, 'Would have no reason to complain of being bullied and that they would have good times as any they had at present'.[8] Setting aside the omission that good times in the army would include being shot at, the mention of bullying must have been raised to address a genuine concern in the farming community.

Contemporary newspaper reports show that due to heavy rain much of the route march was cancelled. Instead, on Friday, the men travelled by train from Duns to Earlston. The *Berwickshire Advertiser* reported that during the march:

> The various halting places appeals had been made to young men to join the battalion either for home or foreign service, but at Earlston there was no opportunity for such an appeal, and indeed it was not needed here for Earlston had contributed her quota to the ranks in measure, but elsewhere, the country districts young men are holding back strangely, apparently not realizing the great need of the country in defending her liberties and providing safety of her existence.[9]

When the war was declared, there was a surge of men wanting to enlist. After two months, 40 per cent of eligible men in the village had joined up. There must have been a mix of reasons why someone would sign up so readily: patriotism, a sense of adventure, peer pressure would have been among them. Defeat would have been unthinkable. Great Britain was, after all, a huge military power. No wonder so many thought that the war would be over by Christmas. One thing that would not have driven men to give up their jobs to join the military was money, and this was particularly true of poorly paid agriculture jobs.

Newspapers of the day show that ploughmen were being hired for around 19 shillings a week. In 1914, a private in the infantry was paid around 1 shilling per day, so for a farmhand to enlist would mean a drop in wages of around 50 per cent and, with most farmworkers' wives also employed on farms for lower pay, the loss of income was significant.

The 1914 cost of living can be judged from an announcement made in the *Berwick Advertiser* in October of that year. The Northern

Cyclist Battalion was running a recruitment campaign for a reserve battalion. The announcement advised that potential volunteers would be paid 3 shillings per day, of which 1 shilling was pay and 2 shillings was a subsistence allowance, paid while living at home. So, it can be assumed that the Government determined that the minimum cost of living per person was 2 shillings a day.[10]

However, not all men were reluctant to join up. William Doughty was an Earlston school teacher who may have been influenced by the recruitment campaign when the KOSBs visited the village. In any event, on 9 November he composed a letter to his employers, the Earlston School Board, requesting a leave of absence for the duration of the war, to enlist in the Lothians and Border Horse Yeomanry. Cannily, he asked that the board sanction payment of the difference between his teacher's salary of £100 per annum and his army pay.

When the board met on the following Wednesday, the clerk read out William's letter, and it agreed to meet William's request, noting that an equivalent female teacher could be hired for, 'only £70'.

And so, at 5.20 p.m. on Wednesday, 18 November, William boarded the train to take him to his regiment. According to the *Berwick Advertiser*:

> A number of the school children, who were all deeply attached to their esteemed teacher, assembled at the railway station to take farewell of him and wish him success in his patriotic resolution. The youngsters gave appropriate and pathetic expression of their feelings on the occasion by singing the well-known Scottish song 'Will ye no come back again' – an expression of goodwill in which all Mr Doughty's friends will heartily join.'

William did as he had promised and joined the Lothians and Border Horse Yeomanry as a private. However, and perhaps as a result of the training he had received in the Officer Training Corps of Edinburgh University when studying for his MA, William was promoted 2nd Lieutenant and transferred to the 4th Kings Own Scottish Borders. He earned another promotion to Lieutenant and served in Palestine and France. He was wounded in October 1918, at Cambrai. He returned to Earlston after the war, then, in 1919 was appointed as a master at Daniel Stewart's College in Edinburgh.

Another person who may have been influenced by the recruitment campaign was John Boyd.

On 3 August 1914, British Foreign Secretary, Sir Edward Grey, is said to have remarked that, 'The lamps are going out all over Europe, we shall not see them lit again in our lifetime'. Sir Edward was, of course, referring to Britain's entry into the war. However, at 5 Rodger's Place, Earlston, the home of Philip and Ella Boyd, the flame of patriotism was burning bright. The Boyd's son, John, an apprentice grocer, was determined to do his bit for King and Country.

By the end of October and, no doubt worried by the rumour that the war would be over by Christmas, John presented himself to the recruiting sergeant of the King's Own Scottish Borderers in Galashiels. After a few questions and a brief medical, John swore the oath taken by all recruits on attestation:

> I, John Boyd, swear by Almighty God, that I will be faithful and bear true Allegiance to His Majesty King George the Fifth, His Heirs, and Successors, and that I will, as duty bound, honestly and faithfully defend His Majesty, His Heirs, and Successors, in Person, Crown and Dignity against all enemies, according to the conditions of my service.

And with that John Boyd, grocer's apprentice, became Boyd, John, Private, 8276, King's Own Scottish Borderers. That was until three weeks after enlisting when the army discovered that John was only 16 years old and he was discharged from the army, his papers noting that he was, 'Discharged having made a misstatement as to age on enlistment'.

For the time being, John's only enemy would be angry customers at the grocer's shop, and his most dangerous action would be cleaning the bacon slicer. But the war would not be over by Christmas, and so John would get his chance to serve – an honour that would cost him his life.

Thomas Young, the son of village bootmaker Archibald Young, had joined the Army Service Corps. He was stationed in Hartlepool in December when the town was bombarded by the three German heavy cruisers *Blucher*, *Sydlitz* and *Moltke* at around 8 a.m. on 16 December.

The bombardment killed 112 people and wounded over 200 others. That a town full of innocent men, women and children had been targeted caused outrage. Stories that a church had been hit, a school shelled, and that a family of five, the Bennetts, were killed eating breakfast when a shell struck their house, fuelled hatred towards the Germans.

Thomas wrote a letter to his mother describing how he saw, 'Poor mothers carrying their poor little bairns to the hospital to be attended to, the blood running off them'. His letter also pointed to another concern. He told his mother that, 'The worst of it all is that the German cruisers seem to be still knocking about our coast, as a scare was started yesterday that they were here again and we were all warned by the police to go away into the country as far as we could get for our own safety.' There was public concern that Great Britain, with 'the mightiest navy in the world', was unable to defend citizens of an English coastal town.

In closing his letter, Thomas told his mother: 'I am sending you and father some pieces of shell, they are only small bits, but they will be treasures for you because they are part of the first shells to be fired on the British coast.'[11]

Thomas survived the shelling and the war, although his brothers, Robert and George, would be killed.

Chapter 2

1915

With the war only a few months old, the insatiable need for recruits was championed by newspapers nationwide, with the 'Clarion call for men and yet more men'.

Local newspapers took up the cause by reporting on a county, parish and town basis. The numbers published did not stand up to any scrutiny since the percentages quoted were not based on the number of men of military age, but rather on the number of men, women and children of all ages. For example, Earlston was reported as having recruited just over 7 per cent. However, taking into account only men of military age, 40 per cent of Earlston's menfolk had enlisted.

For the newspaper proprietors, it may have been a case of the ends justifying the means.

It was Rudyard Kipling who suggested that, 'Their bodies are buried in peace, but their name liveth for evermore' should be inscribed on war memorials (Ecclesiasticus 44:14). However, Sir Edward Luytens, the architect and designer of the Commonwealth War Graves Commission cemeteries and memorials, was concerned that someone would inadvertently include an 's' at the end of 'peace'.

A compromise was reached by agreeing that only 'Their name liveth for evermore' would be quoted.

This proved insightful in several ways. Many family headstones in church cemeteries fall into disrepair. Cemeteries are becoming overcrowded, and in some, family plots are 'recycled' after three generations. The names of the War dead are inscribed on memorials such as the Menin Gate, or headstones like those at Tyne Cot Cemetery, and these are kept in immaculate condition by the Commonwealth War Graves Commission, as are the grounds. These are not allowed to fall into disrepair or be 'recycled'. Also, men who died of natural causes when serving are remembered. As we shall see, three men who died of pneumonia have their names inscribed next to those killed in action or who died from wounds. Pneumonia was a common cause of death in the early twentieth century, but very few of those who succumbed to the infection will be remembered 100 years after their death. Not so for the men serving their country. Their names will live on for evermore.

Earlston's first fatality was James Archibald, the son of James and Robina Archibald who ran a bakery on Earlston's High Street.

James was very popular in the village. He drove his father's bread van and so had a wide circle of acquaintances. He had been in the Territorials for two years before the war was declared and immediately volunteered for foreign service. On Thursday, 6 August 1914, Archibald, together with about 50 other Territorials, marched from Earlston to Galashiels before taking the train to the King's Own Scottish Borderers garrison in Cambusbarron for basic training.

In February the following year, he was granted a short leave. When he was at home, his mother noticed that he had developed a cough and, as any concerned mother would do, suggested that James visit Dr Young for a remedy. James, however, being a teenager (he was only 18) and not wishing to be delayed getting back to his regiment, ignored his mother's advice.

On his return to his regiment, he was able to perform all his regular duties, albeit that he was hoarse. However, one morning his commanding officer, concerned for his health had him transferred to the garrison's temporary hospital.

Initially, James was making good progress, but by Sunday, 14 February his condition deteriorated. At about midday his parents received a telephone message from Captain Sharpe, saying that he was seriously ill and in about half an hour, in a second message, they were informed that he had died.

Later that day Captain Sharpe wrote to James's parents:

Dear Mr Archibald,

It is with deep regret that I have, to inform you of the death of your son this morning. He has had a bit of cold hanging about him for a little while I believe, but nothing more than the usual run, like most of us, have had. On Thursday, however, was taken to a room reserved for the sick and laid up influenza. I know what a blow this will be to Mrs Archibald and yourself, and I can only extend to you heartfelt sympathy. James was a good boy and since came here has done his best to prepare himself to fight for his King and Country, and a credit to you all. He has been called early in the fight, but try to find some consolation in the fact that he has laid down his life for his King and Country just as much if he had been laid low by an enemy's bullet on the plains of Flanders. He was doing quite well, and this morning he had quite a good breakfast and was in his usual cheery form. Shortly afterwards, however, he took suddenly ill and soon became unconscious. There were two doctors in attendance, and I can assure you that everything was done that could be done: but he was beyond their help, and passed away about 11.15 a.m. I am sure he suffered no pain as became unconscious almost as soon as the serious turn came on, and from then onwards I was with him, along with the doctors, and he never regained consciousness. He is in the mortuary at Stirling Castle, but I hope you will come here first, and let me know when you arrive so that I can meet you and make the necessary arrangements. He will get a military funeral here, but I am sure you will wish to take him home Earlston, where private arrangements will have to be made.

I am, yours sincerely,
Robert W. Sharpe Captain, 4th KOSB.[12]

Mrs Archibald travelled to Stirling on the following Monday to make the necessary arrangements for the funeral. A military funeral was conducted when James's body was transferred from Stirling Castle to the railway station. The train arrived in Earlston in the late afternoon. Men from the regiment, including Sergeant Louis Fisher, travelled on the same train. The following day a large crowd of mourners gathered at the Archibald's house for a short service before the funeral cortège made its way along the High Street to Earlston Parish churchyard (Figure 5). The hearse was flanked by Sergeant Fisher and a private on one side, and Colour Sergeant Wilkie and a private on the other.

Nobody that day could have predicted that the next military funeral at the churchyard would be Colour Sergeant Wilkie's.

Figure 5. James Archibald's grave in Earlston churchyard.

During a speech given in August 1914, Colonel Hope had urged that, 'Opponents should not be abused. ... Britons', he said, to much applause, 'had the greatest confidence in their army, in their generals, and in the way, they were going into the fight. They should not despise their enemies, because it was well known that they are strong, that they are good fighters, and that there are a great many of them.'

These were noble sentiments, but news from Europe soon caused public outrage. Atrocities carried out by some Germans soldiers when they invaded Belgium earned them the nickname 'Baby Killers'. In May, the *Jedburgh Gazette* carried a report from an officer in the Seaforth Highlanders in which he stated that:

> Those brutes of Germans. They squirted petrol over our wounded and then tried to set them on fire. A few men were burnt, but, fortunately, some were already dead. One of the 1st Battalion was lying wounded out in front, and he went on fire. Another man rushed out amid a hail of bullets, lay down beside him, took his clothes off, stood up and stamped out the fire, bandaged him up, and then got back to the trench.[13]

Perhaps the event that caused the most outrage both nationally and internationally, at least in neutral countries such as the United States of America was the execution of Edith Cavell.

Cavell was a British nurse who was in Belgium at the outbreak of war training Belgian nurses. The training college became a Red Cross Hospital and treated civilians and troops. In 1914, Cavell was asked to assist two British soldiers to escape back to the British sector. This she did, and over the next few months helped more than 200 British, French and Belgian troops escape. Additionally, Cavell sent secret intelligence to the British. Eventually, she and around thirty others involved in the network were arrested by the German authorities and tried by court martial. She was found guilty of spying and executed by firing squad in October 1915.

The British Government was quick to seize the opportunity and capitalize on her death, and recruitment posters started to appear with a portrait photograph of Cavell and the banner headline of 'Murdered by the Hun'. Using this photo, men were urged to enlist.

Fortunately, there was some news to cheer the villagers. In February the *Berwick Advertiser* covered a story under the heading, 'An Earlston Mascot for the Army'. The article tells that Archibald Paterson (who would have been around five years old) had a 'very intelligent dog which rejoices in the name of Laddie, a cross between a collie and an Airedale'.[14] It appears that Archibald's father thought that the dog might be suitable for military purposes. Samuel Fisher, a member of the village recruitment committee, contacted Major Richardson, the well-known breeder and trainer of dogs for the army, and offered him the dog. Major Richardson in reply, telegraphed instructions that the animal be dispatched immediately like any other recruit, with its own railway bill. And so Laddie was sent off to do his bit for King and Country. It is not known if Laddie survived.

Concerns were being raised in the press about public health. The variable winter weather had given rise to the usual ailments, with the elderly particularly susceptible to influenza, pneumonia and lumbago, whereas young children suffered from whooping cough, measles and bronchitis. However, soldiers were returning home from basic training suffering from various ailments or carrying diseases from their garrisons. The death of John Archibald was fresh in everyone's memory.

Colonel Hope had, in his August speech, talked about the country getting help from the colonies. Henry Forbes was an ex-Earlston resident who had emigrated to Canada and had 'answered the call'.
Henry Forbes was born on 11 October 1884, in Methlick, Aberdeenshire. In the 1890s Henry and his parents, Arthur and Mary Forbes moved to Gordon, Berwickshire, where Arthur was employed as a forester on the Mellerstain Estate. Henry trained as a plumber, and for whatever reason, decided to emigrate to Canada.
He travelled to Liverpool and boarded the SS *Virginian*. The ship arrived in Quebec on 3 June 1910, and Henry gained a job as a Water Inspector with the Canadian Pacific Railroad before enlisting.

On 24 September 1914, in Valcartier, Henry joined the 72nd Seaforth Highlanders before transferring to the 16th, then the 17th Battalion Canadian Infantry. He shipped to Europe on 3 October 1914, as part of the Canadian Expeditionary Force

On 23 April he sustained a shrapnel wound to his leg and was evacuated to the No. 1 Stationary Casualty Clearing Station in Rouen, where he died of his wounds on 27 April 1915. He is buried in Hazebrouck Communal Cemetery and remembered on the village war memorial.

Earlston's next casualty was Alexander Milne. Alexander was born in the Gorbals of Glasgow in 1889. Alexander's mother, Henrietta (née Cormack) had died of tuberculosis in 1895 aged 27. In 1897, his father married again: Isabella Williamson was born and raised in the Shetland Islands and was only 17 years old – a mere 11 years older than Alexander.

His father, Malcolm, moved the family to Earlston, where Alexander finished his schooling and became an apprentice with Tom Murdison, slater and plumber, who described Alexander as one of the cleverest youngsters he ever had in his service.

In 1905, Alexander joined the King's Own Scottish Borderers, 1st Battalion, and saw three years' service in Egypt, followed by five years in India, rising to the rank of Colour Sergeant Major.

The battalion was in Lucknow, India, when war was declared, and so it was ordered to return to Britain, arriving on 28 December 1914.

Many young men were enlisting in the army now and, in Earlston, patriotism ran high. The King's Own Scottish Borderers was the local regiment, with a long and proud history, so it was natural that many men joined the 4th Battalion (Territorial).

Naturally, this was an anxious time for the mothers of men who had enlisted. We don't know whether other mothers would have sought words of comfort and reassurance from Isabella Milne, or whether they would have considered her an outsider and too young.

However, the fact that her stepson had been in the KOSB's for nine years and had been safe all that time must have made her appear knowledgeable.

With Turkey entering the war and siding with Germany, the British Government decided to invade Turkey at a place called Gallipoli. The 1st Battalion KOSB was one of the many battalions that made up the invasion force. On 18 March 1915, the KOSBs left Avonmouth for Alexandria, Egypt, on board the SS *Dongola*. On arrival in Alexandria, Egypt, the 1st Battalion transferred to the SS *Southland* and arrived in Mudros Bay, Greece, on 18 April.

In Mudros Bay every man practised disembarkation by rope ladder. The role of the 1st Battalion was to provide a diversionary attack at a landing beach in Gallipoli and boat-to-boat transfer was a vital element of the plan.

The SS *Southland* left Mudros Bay on 24 April to rendezvous with ships of the Royal Navy. The 1st Battalion moved to HMS *Amethyst* and HMS *Sapphire*. These warships steamed towards Gallipoli and the landing beaches, where they rendezvoused with some fishing trawlers. The men transferred to the fishing trawlers, which then made their way to the landing beaches under cover of darkness on 25 April. The trawlers towed boats and when in reach of the shore, the soldiers clambered into the boats and rowed ashore.

Once on shore, the plan started to unravel since maps of the area were inaccurate; entrenching tools were not available forcing the men to take shelter behind their packs; dust and sand caused the rifles to jam; and the regiments of the Brigade used different sized bullets hence men quickly ran out of ammunition. This last issue forced men to resort to hand-to-hand fighting.

The phrase 'hand-to-hand fighting' does not convey the savagery of this action. The book, *The K.O.S.B. in the Great War*, describes one incident as follows:

> Private J. Sweeney, an Iro-Scot from Gorebridge, dashed into a group of Turks, bayoneted two, lost his rifle, and emulating the famous Sir Edward Cameron of Lochiel, by fastening his teeth in a Turk's throat, receiving a wound that eventually proved mortal.[15]

On 29 April all surviving troops were ordered to return to the navy ships, their diversionary attack having been completed.

Alexander did not survive but was killed in action some time on 26 April. His remains were never recovered and he is remembered with honour at the Helles Memorial.

In 1908, Earlston Rhymers Football Club organized an Old Year's Night dance at the Earlston Corn Exchange. The music was provided by the Hewitt Band, made up of Adam Hewitt, Adam Kerr and David Hogg. When the bells rang in 1909 and 'Auld Lang Syne' had been sung, there was a break to allow the partygoers and the band members to do some *first footin'* before resuming the celebrations.

The intermission perhaps gave Adam Hewitt time to reflect on the preceding year and to contemplate the forthcoming one. His eldest son John was doing particularly well. A little less than eighteen months before, the *Southern Reporter* newspaper had published an article about His Majesty's Inspector's report of Earlston Public School, which included the marks achieved by the school's top four performers. John's name was top of the list.

The newspaper carried another article about a meeting of the School Board at which Colonel Hope had presided, in which it was reported that in the examination of candidates for the Wilson Bursary, conducted by Mr Robert Martin, John Hewitt had achieved the highest marks and therefore had been appointed Bursar. Consequently, John was able to attend the High School in Duns and receive a higher level in education.

In 1910, John travelled to Edinburgh to sit the Civil Service exam. Passing this would provide John with a secure future working as a civil servant. Almost 800 candidates took the exam and John was placed in 132nd position. His future looked bright.

He left school as soon as he could without finishing the academic year. Such was his popularity that the School Board waived the requirement that the unused portion of his bursary be returned.

John left his home in Rodger's Place, in Earlston, as well as his parents Adam and Agnes Hewitt and brothers Robert and James, and travelled to Dundee to take up his new position in the Civil Service (Figure 6).

Figure 6. John Hewitt who died during the attack on Aubers Ridge. (Public domain)

In 1912, John passed another Civil Service exam which promoted him to Second Class Clerk, and transferred from Dundee to London, to work in Labour Exchanges created by the National Insurance Act.

In 1914 when war was declared, he joined the 1st/13th Kensington Battalion of the London Regiment, nicknamed the 'Civil Service Regiment'.

His regiment shipped to Le Havre on 4 November 1914, to relieve the 2nd Berkshire two weeks later. The Kensingtons suffered their first casualties the following day.

In the early morning of 9 May 1915, the Kensingtons took part in an assault on German positions, in an action that became known as the 'Battle of Aubers'. A heavy bombardment started at 4.30 a.m., with the intent of 'softening' German positions by using high explosive shells on the German trenches and shrapnel shells to cut the German barbed wire.

From the outset problems occurred. Many British shells fell short, some landing on British trenches and some behind where troops had assembled. At 5 a.m., John's regiment was ordered 'over the top' to attack the German trenches, which were only 100–200 yards away.

The Kensingtons made good progress and managed to achieve their objectives. However, elsewhere the attack was going badly. The fire across No Man's Land was now so intense that officers in the field considered it impossible to continue the assault. German prisoners started flooding towards the British trenches and were mistaken for an attacking force. Confusion ruled. Brigadier General Lowry Cole, the commander of the 25th Division, climbed on to the parapet of the British trenches to restore order and was immediately fatally wounded by enemy fire.

General Haig, on hearing of the breakdown of the attack, ordered a bayonet charge for 8 p.m. Fortunately, the roads and communication trenches were so clogged by men and equipment that the bayonet charge was called off. Only then did senior officers visit the field and finally grasp the situation. A meeting of commanders was scheduled the following day to develop a plan for a second attack.

The troops who had been successful in reaching German lines were forced to retreat due to the lack of support. The last of the Kensingtons made it back to the British trenches by 3 a.m. on 10 May.

Before the planning meeting could take place, word was received that general command in London had diverted shells needed for the second attack to the Dardanelles. The second attack was cancelled.

John's remains were never recovered from the battlefield. He is remembered with honour at the Ploegsteert Memorial, and in perpetuity on the Earlston war memorial.

The butcher's bill for the Battle of Aubers was 11,000 British casualties, most killed within yards of their own trench. No gains were made. His captain wrote to John's parents praising his courage, keenness, cheerfulness and devotion to duty. The reporter of the *Berwickshire News* did not have the same grasp of reality and reported that, 'He died a glorious death fighting for King and Country'.

It took three days for all the British casualties to move through the Field Ambulances. One commentator noted that: 'Mile for mile, Division for Division, this was one of the highest rates of loss during the entire war. There is no memorial to the attack at Aubers Ridge'.[16]

Back in Earlston at the beginning of May, the Edinburgh Central Recruiting Committee had started a recruitment campaign in the Borders, specifically targeting agricultural workers. The *Berwick Advertiser* reported that:

> The caravan, which is drawn by one horse, is profusely covered with striking advertisements, which strongly appealed to the patriotism the agricultural population.

> The travels commenced Earlston on Monday, and the route was by Smailholm, Makerston, Stichel, Ednam and Roxburgh, the week's journey ended at Kelso on Saturday, where a meeting was held on the Square. The principal speaker for the week was Mr J. Golder, JP Loanhead.[17]

The report did not indicate if the campaign had proved successful.

At the outbreak of the war, the British army owned about 25,000 horses. Within two weeks that number had grown to 165,000, following a compulsory purchase order on all horses.

By 1917, the British army had almost 500,000 horses and 250,000 mules. The animals were purchased from the USA, Australia, New Zealand, Spain and Portugal. Some wild horses from the USA were rounded up on the plains and had to be broken by squadron 'rough riders'. The Army Service Corps had previously established Remount Depots when the Remount Squadrons had been formed many years earlier.

The Remount Squadrons were tasked with supplying horses and mules to the front-line divisions. As such, the squadrons procured, trained and shipped the animals to wherever they were needed. The Army Service Corp preferred mature men to be enlisted into the squadrons, and Earlston man, William Graham, fitted the requirements perfectly.

William was brought up around horses. His father was a groom, and so from an early age, William had developed an understanding and confidence with the animals. He lived with his family in Annan, and when he married Annie Gordon, a local girl, in 1906, they continued to live in the area.

By 1915, William and Annie, together with their daughters Agnes (born 1909) and Winnifred (born 1914), had moved to

Redpath, a village just outside Earlston. William was employed as a groom by Colonel Hope at Cowdenknowes.

On Thursday, 11 February 1915, William travelled to Galashiels to enlist in the Army Service Corps, and was immediately transferred to a Remount Squadron. Six weeks later, on 27 March, he was on a ship bound for Egypt as part of the British Egypt Expeditionary Force.

Three months later, William was admitted to the military hospital on 29 June, complaining of diarrhoea, sickness and abdominal pain. He was tested for enteric fever, but the result was negative. He was prescribed rest, diet and astringents. On 6 July his condition deteriorated rapidly and he was diagnosed with general peritonitis. The surgical team examined him but concluded that surgery was not recommended. He died at 5.30 p.m. that day. A post mortem revealed that William died from acute enteritis, a perforated intestine and general peritonitis.

William's body was interred at Alexandria Military and War Memorial Cemetery.

Like all war widows, Annie Graham received a memorial scroll from the army. In acknowledging its receipt, she noted: 'The memorial scroll in memory of my late husband will be highly treasured. Thank you for sending it. Yours truly. Mrs Annie Graham.'

Annie and her daughters left the Earlston area and moved to Silloth, Cumbria, to be with her family.

William wasn't a local man and had lived in the Earlston area for a comparatively short time, and yet his name is commemorated on the war memorial.

So far, 1915 had been a disastrous year, with Earlston losing so many men. But it was about to get worse.

The Battle of Loos was fought between 15 September and 15 October 1915, on land near the city of Lens. Close to the Belgium border, the area was the industrial heartland of north-east France, with many mining villages and collieries. The battle was significant because this was the first large-scale battle of 1915 (6 Divisions), deploying Kitchener's 'New Army'. The battle took place in an area not of British choosing and so, to increase the likelihood of success, the British elected to use poisonous gas for the first time.

Poor leadership allowed the battle to commence before adequate stocks of ammunition and heavy artillery pieces were in place. The casualty rate was shocking, with almost 50,000 killed, wounded or missing in the first attack, with another 8,000 (out of a force of 10,000) killed, wounded or missing in the first four hours of the second attack.

Over three days in late September 1915, four men from Earlston from four regiments died in the battle.

Alexander Fairley, a Lance Corporal with the Black Watch, had spent the night sharing his trench with the gas canisters. He was a ploughman who could walk all day and never tire, but not on that day. On command, each man put on their gas mask. The masks, officially known as Tube Helmets, were crude however they did offer a degree of protection from some of the gases used at the time (Figure 7). The helmet had two layers of flannelette; the outer layer was impregnated with chemicals to neutralize the effects of the gas. The inner layer offered the wearer protection from burns from the chemicals in the outer layer. Two mica lenses and a breathing tube wee fixed to the front of the helmet. The wearers would tuck the lower edge of the helmet under their tunics in a position where, hopefully, they could see out of the eye pieces. They would breathe in air 'filtered' by the chemicals on the outer later, and exhale through the breathing tube. The tube had a valve to prevent gas being drawn into the helmet.

*Figure 7. Soldier wearing a PH or Tube Helmet.
(Licensor: www.awm.gov.au (P03063.007))*

The four days of shelling that had preceded the attack had failed to cut the German barbed wire defences or 'soften up' the German trenches. Instead, the shelling had depleted supplies of ammunition and consequently the advancing British troops did not have the protection of the bombardment during the attack.

And so, with the breathing tube clamed in his mouth and straining to see through the mica lenses, Alexander started his attack on the German lines. The wind that morning was fickle. The exploding British gas cannisters formed thick clouds, obscuring the attackers from German machine gunners and making it difficult for the attackers to find their way across no-man's land. Then the wind would freshen, dispersing the gas clouds, revealing the attackers to the German defenders. As one historian noted, the German machine gunners were *'dumbfounded ... instead of advancing in waves, the British were marching ... some as if on parade ... toward them in ten columns gradually filling no-man's land'*. The German machine gunners were kept busy. One machine gun crew reportedly fired over 12,000 rounds that day.

When the British troops realised that they could proceed no further since the German defences were intact and impenetrable, the men started making their way back to the British lines (Figure 8). The Germans stopped firing to allow the men to retreat and German doctors and medics entered no-man's land to tend to the British wounded.

Eight thousand British troops were killed that day. The Germans named the battlefield the *'Leichenfeld von Loos'* – the *'Corpse field of Loos'*.

The 9th Battalion Black Watch sustained 680 casualties, of which 20 were officers. Alexander was one of these casualties.

James Thomson was one of about 300 villagers who worked at the Simpson and Fairbairn tweed mill in Earlston. His family lived in nearby Galashiels, but James moved to Earlston for employment. But his work now was like nothing he'd experienced before. That September morning, his day started at 6.30 a.m., signalled, not by the mill siren, but by the officer's whistle to leave the trench, when James – now a private in the 6th KOSB – started the attack to capture German trenches with the rest of his battalion of about 800 men.

The attack was only partially successful. The German shells, machine guns, rifle fire and effects of the British gas attack took a heavy toll. And it was only 9.30 a.m. A second attack was ordered against other trenches, but this too failed.

The rest of the day was spent carrying the dead and wounded back to the British trenches.

When the work for that day was done, the battalion had suffered 650 casualties: 201 killed, including James; 169 missing; 274 wounded; and 6 gassed – a terrible tally for a day's labour.

William Stirling had enlisted in Kelso, possibly to avoid his uncle, Samuel Fisher, who was on the Attestation Committee in Earlston. Samuel Fisher was also William's father's boss.

William joined the Cameron Highlanders whereas his cousin, Louis Fisher, had joined the King's Own Scottish Borderers and been wounded in Gallipoli a few months earlier in July.

Unlike his father Charles, uncle Samuel or cousin Louis, William was not a painter and decorator, but instead, worked for Ralph Dodds, the owner of one of the village grocery shops.

In France, William, now a private in the 6th Cameron Highlanders, arrived at the battlefield with his battalion at the end of a long overnight march. Instead of getting some rest, his battalion was immediately pressed into service. The men couldn't get anything to eat since someone had decided that the field kitchens would not be needed and had therefore been moved to the rear. Sustenance was provided by hot tea issued at about 3 a.m., before they moved up to the firing line a couple of hours later.

The men dug a communication trench to get closer to the German lines before the attack proper. By 9.30 a.m. the battalion moved forward in attack and remained in action all that day and through the night, until it was relieved at 5 a.m. the next day, when it marched back to the billets.

The battalion of exhausted men had lost over 400 of their comrades, including William.

Figure 8. German trench barbed wire entanglements. The bombardment failed to cut the barbed wire. (Licensor: www.awm.gov.au (E01655))

The land where the Battle of Loos took place was as flat as a millpond with only two features. There was a small hill of rocks, just dirt really, that William Wilson, a private in the Scots Guards, was told that the miners had dug out of the ground in their quest for coal. And then there was the tall metal structure of the pit winding gear to move the miners up and down to the coal face. Some of the English troops called it 'Tower Bridge' because it looked like the bridge in London. William must have wondered why anyone would fight over this piece of land.

He hadn't been in the army that long, but he knew enough about soldiering to realize that this was not a good place. It was just so flat. Anyone above ground level could be seen from miles around – not good when there were snipers and machine gunners intent on killing them.

William, like his father and brothers, was a shepherd. Growing up and working in the Cheviot and Lammermuir Hills, he was used to hilly country and his body had adapted itself to the demanding terrain. Spending days walking up and down hills, sometimes carrying a stray yearling lamb, toughened a man.

In winter, working in piercing wind and driving snow, at times walking through waist-deep snowdrifts to find missing sheep, he could always find a dip in the ground that offered some shelter. But there was no shelter at Loos from piercing shells and bullets.

In the Borders on summer days, the scenery was magnificent, with the rolling hills and the greenery of the woods and crops in the fields. Here, there was nothing like that. Going over the top, William could have sprinted over the ground to the enemy's trenches without losing breath. Instead, he had to keep pace with the creeping barrage set by the gunners. He strolled towards oblivion.

Between 25 and 30 September, the 1st Battalion Scots Guards sustained 444 casualties, including William.

In Earlston, despite these tragic events, life went on. The village public school was forced to close due to an outbreak of measles. Meantime the region was suffering a particularly hard winter. The hard frosts meant that much of the outdoor work was brought to a standstill. However, skating on the Georgefield curling pond proved very popular, and the light from the full moon enabled skating to continue into the evening.

James Notman is remembered on the Earlston war memorial as a private in the Camerons, although he enlisted in the Army Service Corps (ASC). In the Earlston section of the *Southern Reporter*, on Thursday, 3 June 1915, it was announced: 'Recruiting – Last week there were attested in Earlston … James Notman, Army Service Corps (ASC: Horse Transport Department)'.

James was born in Legerwood on 5 June 1896, the son of Alexander and Susan Notman. Susan developed Bright's Disease and died on 13 July 1896, when James was barely five weeks old. Consequently, he lived with his grandparents, James and Christina Notman, and his sister Christina, who was nineteen years his senior, who acted as a surrogate mother.

All of James's family were 'farm servants' with the men being ploughmen. So, James's choice of joining the Army Service Corp Horse Transport Department seems natural. However, his time in the ASC was short. His entries in the Medal Index Cards show that he transferred from the ASC to the Cameron Highlanders 1/5th Battalion on 1 October, 1915.

Each infantry battalion had a headquarters, which included specialist roles such as signallers, drivers, pioneers, and so on. From 1914, infantry battalions had horses assigned: 13 riding horses; 26 draught horses; 8 heavy draught horses; and 9 pack horses. The draught and pack horses had to pull a range of carts and wagons which contained the battalion's equipment. Hence each battalion needed men with James's horse skills.

His new service number, S/18499, carried the 'S' to denote that the wearer was from ASC, but had been recruited into the aptly numbered Kitchener Army.

James was killed on 27 November 1915, less than two months after joining the Camerons. He is buried in Railway Dugouts Burial Ground, about one mile from Komenseweg, in Belgium. His death was announced in the *Edinburgh Evening News* on 4 December, although the *Berwickshire News and General Advertiser* was still reporting James as being alive in December.[18]

Chapter 3

1915: Achi Baba Nullah

The war in Gallipoli continued and one battle in particular affected so many Earlston families that it deserves attention.

In June 1915, the 4th and 5th Battalions, King's Own Scottish Borderers (KOSBs), were resting in preparation for an attack. The target was the Turkish trenches in an area called Achi Baba Nullah. Reconnaissance had reported what appeared to be a new trench behind two previously dug trenches. The objective of the attack was to overrun the first and second Turkish trenches, then consolidate the new, third trench (Figure 9). The attack took place under a rolling barrage from the Allied naval guns. The range of the guns was adjusted, creeping towards, and then over, the Turkish positions, allowing the infantry to advance under its cover.

A Village at War

GALLIPOLI

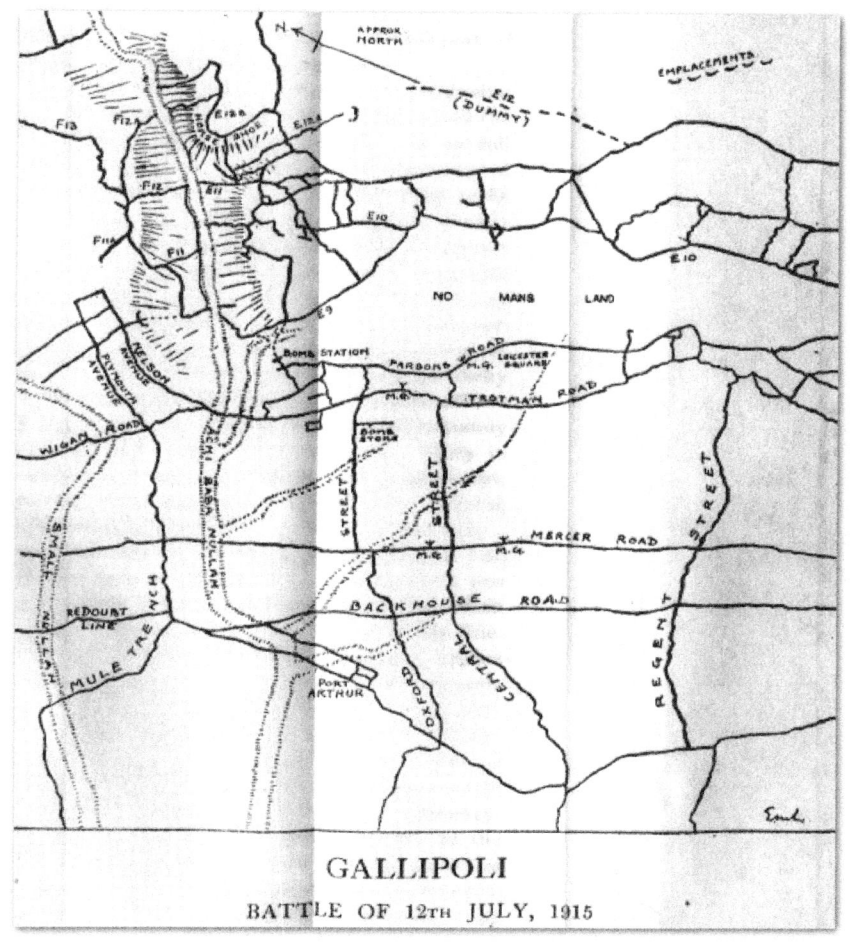

BATTLE OF 12TH JULY, 1915

Figure 9. Map of Achi Baba Nullah. D Company's objective is shown at the top of the map as a broken line, marked 'Dummy' (Public domain)

On 29 June the battalion War Diary notes, 'Casualties to date, one officer wounded, seven men killed and 36 wounded'.[19] This toll, it turned out, was the quiet before the storm.

It is not known just how many men of the 4th Battalion took part in the attack (a battalion strength was between 650 and 1,000 men), nor how many were Earlstonians, but the names and fate of some Earlstonians are known.

Sergeant Louis (aka 'Lewis') Fisher was NCO of D Company. He was wounded in the shoulder and treated at Casualty Hospital W Beach before being transferred to a hospital in Cairo.

William Kerr survived unscathed.

Brothers Henry and William Turnbull, sons of James and Mary (née Cunninghma) took part in the attack. The family lived on Mill Road in Earlston and James' occupation is variously listed as contactor, farmer and miller.

During the attack Henry was wounded and taken prisoner. He, along with eleven fellow KOSBs were taken to Kiangri prison in Turkey. Two other men from the 4th Battalion were captured and imprisoned in Constantinople.

William was born in Earlston in 1887 and before the war he was employed as a lorry man with the North British Railway. In 1912, he married Elizabeth Cunningham, a millworker, who lived at The Terrace, which forms part of Earlston High Street. Their daughter, Mary Cunningham Turnbull, was born on 30 May 1913. A son, James Cunningham Turnbull, was born on 31 December 1914, but died ten days later from bronchitis. His mother, Elizabeth, had died five days earlier from pneumonia. William's military records show that he had a son who was born in 1907, although no other records of the birth can be traced.

In 1922, the army contacted William's father requesting confirmation of details of 'the soldier's relatives now living'. On the form (Army Form W. 5080) James wrote that William had a son, William Elliot, born on 18 May 1907. The child was now living with James and his wife at 'Lindean' in Earlston, whereas his daughter was living with her aunt, Isabella Kerr, at Temple House, West Linton, Peeblesshire.

William sustained a bullet wound to his forehead and he was taken to the rest camp. He was transferred to the Casualty Hospital on 'W' Beach but died of his wounds on 15 July. He is buried at Lancashire Landing Cemetery.

Privates James and John Bell, ploughmen from Fans Farm, were wounded.

William Aikman, a sergeant in the 4th Battalion, died. His twin brother Henry and younger brother John, also served with the regiment (Figure 10). When William's death was announced, different people remembered him in different ways. Those people he worked with at the Simpson and Fairbairn tweed mill recalled him as one of the power loom tuners who kept the looms in working order. Members of the Lodge of Rechabites remembered being entertained by William with his collection of gramophone records, and he was remembered as a good golfer by members of the Earlston Golf Club and a winner of several trophies such as the Wallace Challenge Cup and other competitions. People also recalled his love of whist drives, especially those in aid of a good cause such as the fundraiser for the 'Back Road Improvement' proposal. Fellow members of the Territorials recalled his marksmanship on the Black Hill rifle range, where he had been successful in several competitions.

Figure 10. The Aikman brothers. From left to right: John, Henry and William. (Source: Sheila MacKay)

Privates W. Harkness and Adam Scott survived, but were initially reported missing.

Alexander Cessford did not survive. He was born in Lauder, Berwickshire, in 1892, the son of William and Jane Cessford. Alexander lived with his parents on the High Street until he moved to Galashiels, working as a mule piecer at a local woollen mill.

Brothers William and Andrew Brockie were wounded. Andrew was injured in the eye and transferred to the Royal Infirmary in Edinburgh for treatment.

John Hardie was killed. He lived on the High Street with his parents, John and Charlotte, and siblings. Like his father, John and sisters Joan, Isabella, Jane and Betsy worked at Simpson and Fairbairn tweed mill. John was another crack shot on the rifle range and had represented Earlston at the Border Rifle Association.

George Johnston was initially reported as missing then, later, as killed. On the eve of the attack, George felt compelled to write a letter home to his mother. After the attack, the letter was recovered from his body, together with his copy of the New Testament. The book had been pierced by a bullet; most likely the fatal shot. George wrote:

> 11 July
> My Dear Mother,
>
> Just a few lines to say we are having an attack on the 12th, Monday morning, and we are in the first line. If I do happen to go under I hope that this note will be sent on to you and, dear father and mother, if it is my luck, don't vex yourselves, for I intend to do my duty and I will go on to the bitter end. I hope you will never forget the little son who came up when his country called. If I do get through, well and good, but I will trust in my Heavenly Father's strength and guidance.

We have all sinned, and we all look to our Heavenly Father for mercy on us all. Now, dear mother and all. I will close with fondest remembrances

And kindest love.
From your ever-loving son,
George B.

Whoever gets me please address this to my mother, Mrs G. Johnston, Thorn Street, Earlston, Berwickshire, Scotland.

PS. Mind and give Jeanie my fondest love and kindest regards.

From George B.[20]

Robert Young, the son of Archibald and Margaret Young, who lived on the High Street in Earlston, also died. Archibald was a bootmaker, and Robert had followed into his father's trade.

In February 1900 he enlisted in the 2nd Battalion King's Own Scottish Borderers for one year. In 1901, he rejoined the Colours to serve in the South-African war. He was discharged in 1902 and returned to a hero's welcome in Earlston. When Robert and another Earlston soldier, James Maltman (son of Alexander, the village fishmonger), returned to the railway station, they found that schoolchildren had been given permission to leave their classes and mill workers had been given an hour off to join in the celebrations. At a ceremony, both Robert and James were presented with a silver watch and gold watch chain as a memento of their service in South Africa.

On his return to civilian life, James and his family emigrated to Canada in 1904, and settled in Minitonas, Manitoba. There, James met and married Nellie Viola Hart and they raised their son, David. James died in 1953 and is buried in British Columbia.

Robert moved to Edinburgh, plying his trade as a bootmaker to a Mr McGillewie (sic) of Morningside Place, in Edinburgh. On

17 December 1909, Robert married Euphemia Scott, a dressmaker (Figure 11). Five years later Robert enlisted in the 4th Battalion, King's Own Scottish Borderers. As shown, the battalion was deployed to Gallipoli in 1915, where Robert met his death.

Figure 11. Robert and Euphemia Young (Source: Laura MacKenzie)

Robert's widow Euphemia remarried in June 1917, to George Richard McCarthy, an Irishman living in Edinburgh. In 1919, she died in labour, giving birth to twins, neither of whom survived. Her husband emigrated to New Zealand, where he died in 1969.

A Village at War

To understand the events as they unfolded over the days at the end of June, and the attack on 12 July, it is necessary to refer to the battalion's official War Diary, which is quoted here:

> War Diary: 4th Battalion King's
> Own Scottish Borderers
>
> 28 June – Battalion rested preparatory to an attack.
>
> 29 June – Casualties to date, one officer wounded*, seven men killed, and 36 wounded.
>
> 30 June–9 July – Battalion remained at the rest camp, the attack having been postponed. The men were kept busy furnishing fatigue parties for entrenching work.
>
> 10 July – Battalion moved up to Brownhouse and Backhouse Post reserve line trenches.
>
> 11 July – Battalion moved up to Parsons Road and Trotman Road firing line trenches preparatory to an attack. Received orders to attack three lines of Turkish trenches at 7.35 a.m. on 12 July passing over the first and second line and to occupy and consolidate the third line.
>
> 12 July – Bombardment by our artillery on Turkish trenches commenced at 6.55 a.m. At 7.35 a.m. the

---

* The wounded officer was most likely 2nd Lieutenant Robert Smith from Earlston. According to an article in the *Hawick News* on 23 July 1915, Smith sustained a leg wound. He was evacuated to a hospital in Alexandria, Egypt, from where he was able to telegraph his mother, Mrs Dawson-Smith, about his condition.

range of our artillery was lengthened, and the Battalion moved to the attack, passed over the first and second trench and continued advancing with the object of occupying the third trench. After advancing a distance of some 400 to 500 yards Col McNicole who commanded and was at the front leading the Battalion said to me, 'We are too far forward, we must get back'. I replied, 'Very well, sir, I'll stop the men and get them back.' No third trench was seen during the advance or when going back. Casualties were not very heavy during the advance, but when going back the Battalion had to pass through the zone of fire of our own artillery, also the fire from the enemies' artillery, machine-guns and rifles causing heavy losses. We then occupied part of the second Turkish trench which we commenced consolidating.

13 July – Early on the morning of 13th, the enemy delivered a counter–attack, which was repulsed. Fighting continued the greater part of the day. Casualties occurred during the fighting.

14 July – Continued occupying these trenches until orders were received (about 3–4 p.m.) to withdraw Battalion and reorganize at Brownhouse line. Passed night in these lines.

15 July – About 4 p.m. orders were received to take Battalion to rest camp arrived 5–7 p.m.

16 July – Carried on reorganization and compiled lists of casualties as follows – Officers Killed 5 Wounded 6

Missing 7. Total 18. Other ranks Killed 57 Wounded 203 Missing 275. Total 535.

17 July–31 July – Reorganization. Completing equipment, arms and clothing. Furnishing fatigue parties for entrenching.[21]

The survivors must have been wracked with guilt. Guilt for having survived and guilt for having to leave wounded comrades lying in No Man's Land. The screams of the wounded, their calls for rescue and water, must have rung in the survivors' ears for years.

There will always be a period after a military engagement when the numbers and identities of casualties are confused. However, the attack on Achi Babu Nallah seems to have caused a significant breakdown in communications.

For the families in Earlston, the wait must have been excruciating.

On 3 August, the *Berwickshire News* reported William Turnbull had been officially declared killed. His brother, Henry, was reported wounded and a prisoner of the Turks, and was being held in Constantinople. Sergeant Louis Fisher was reported as wounded and hospitalized in Cairo. Two privates named as Bell – possibly James and John Bell, ploughmen at Fans Farm – were reported wounded, as were brothers William and Andrew Brockie.

On 5 August, the *Southern Reporter* published an 'official' list of casualties. The only Earlston name on the list was Private William Brockie, who was reported missing.

Almost a week later, the *Berwickshire News and General Advertiser* published part of a letter written by Louis Fisher to his parents with his account of the charge. Written from the Government Hospital, Kasr-el-Aini, Cairo on 21 July Louis wrote:

> You will be wanting me to give you some account of the charge we made on 12 July and how I got wound.

We made two charges that I know of, although it was reported later, we made three. It was in the second charge I got hit. The morning opened with a furious bombardment against the Turks by our artillery, and that of the French—the best in the world. The orders received were, that the shell fire was to cease at 7.30 a.m. and that we were to be on the Turks at 7.35 a.m., so you see everything was timed. The object was to take three trenches, so that, in our rush, we had two clear out, then jump into the third one. When the signal was given to charge, we jumped up and out of our trenches as quickly possible, each man carrying either a pick or shovel, and his fixed bayonet. With the French on our right, we made the first assault, clearing the trenches quite easily, but to gain a position and hold it are two different things. The French, for reasons of their own, which I will explain later, promptly retired, with the result that the Turkish supports came sweeping over the hill like bees, and forced us to retire under very heavy fire, both from shell and bullet. They also got on our right, where the French had been a few minutes before, and poured in lead on us. The reason the French had retired is because they always do so here, the object being to draw the enemy out, and turn on them in the open; a good enough idea, when working by themselves, but a costly one for us, as we do not care about retiring. After we had retired into our old firing line, the next thing to be done was to charge again. We did so, and the second charge came off as easily as the first, although the shrapnel fire of the Turks was most steady.

It was in the latter charge I was wounded. Just as I jumped the second trench a bullet went through my arm, and forced me to drop my rifle. I immediately got under cover, and put on the first dressing. After that I was left to get out of it as best I could and find the nearest dressing station. It is impossible here to give you a proper idea of what a charge is like, but I may say it is nothing short of pure hell. It seems a funny thing to say, but the noise is so great that you cannot hear it, what with big black shells (coal boxes) bursting on the ground, and shrapnel bursting overhead, to say nothing of the rattle of rifles, and the shouting of men, it is awful. The Turks like it worse than we do. They cannot stand the bayonet, and usually clear out as soon as they see our men advancing.

We have all sorts of troops here including Australians, and different tribes from India, the Ghurkhas being the most prominent among them. We have also some hill tribes, tall, black men with side whiskers, fierce looking men they are; besides Egyptians and Singhalese. They also are tall men.[22]

On 19 August, the *Southern Reporter* carried another 'official' list, in which Private William Turnbull of Earlston was listed as having died from his wounds.

The article carried unofficial lists of names and the status of men thought to be casualties. Such was the scale of the catastrophe that the newspaper lists of the border villages and towns reporting 'missing' men makes pitiable reading: Selkirk, Hawick, Galashiels, St Boswells, Kelso, Jedburgh, Lauder, Langholm, Coldingham, Newcastleton, Morebattle, Leitholm, Synton, Westruther, Grantshouse and Edrom.

From Earlston, George Johnston, A. Scott and W. Harkness were reported as missing.

Over the coming days and months, news of the attack continued to be published. Hopes were raised and dashed, and prayers answered. There were reports that men had rejoined their battalion weeks after the assault, and of the Turks taking prisoners who were shipped to Constantinople.

In a possible attempt to draw a line under the debacle, seven months after the attack, on 24 February 1916, the *Southern Reporter* published two letters relating to the failed Achi Baba Nullah assault, which are reproduced here in full, together with the preface to the letters:

Border Territorials at Gallipoli:
Little Hope for Missing Men

It will be remembered that after the engagement at the Dardanelles on the 12 July last, a large number of Territorials belonging to the 1/4th KOSB drawn from the different Border towns were reported missing and that nothing further has been heard of them since. Some of the parents have been making inquiries in regard to their missing sons, and the following letters which have been received explain themselves, and indicate that there is little hope of any of the missing now turning up:

British Red Cross, and Order of St John
17 February 1916

Dear Sir, With reference to your inquiry for your son, we have received from our office in Alexandria the enclosed general account of the attack made by the KOSBs on 12 July and we fear that we shall not be able to obtain any more news about the men of this

Battalion, as you will see by the account of the action that very few survived. Please accept our deepest sympathy.

Yours faithfully
Louis Mallet

Cairo
21 March 1916
King's Own Scottish Borderers
Catastrophe of 12 July

This Battalion, composed at the time chiefly of men of the 1/4th, formed part of the 52nd Division operating at Cape Hellers. A day or so previous to the above date, a Turkish trench had been spotted by aeroplane, and orders were given to the Borderers, on 11 July that they were to take it the following morning. They were also informed that there were two other trenches intervening between themselves and their objective, but that they were weakly held, and that if opposition were offered it would have easily been brushed aside. The trench which the Borderers occupied was between 300 and 400 yards from those which they were going to attack. The plan that was given to them was roughly as indicated below:

From the Scottish Borderers' Trench to the 1st Intervening Trench – 100 yards

From 1st Intervening Trench to the 2nd Intervening Trench – 100 yards

From the 2nd Intervening Trench to the Turkish trench – 150 yards

It was decided that the attack should be delivered by two companies at a time, probably by A and B and supported by C and D but of the actual details my informant was uncertain. In the event, the first two companies jumped over the parapet, successfully stormed the two intervening trenches, and found themselves not long afterwards in the trench which they had been ordered to take. Unfortunately, this proved to be no real trench at all. It was either a dummy trench which had been carefully prepared by the enemy or a fold in the ground which they knew would serve equally well. On arrival they were subjected to terrific fire from rifles and machine-guns. There was no shelter, and they began to fall rapidly. Eventually, a few survivors began to trickle back.

When this was seen by the officer Commanding the two companies who were in support, he immediately gave the order for them to advance without knowing what had occurred. They accordingly rushed forward, caught up the stragglers, with them, and the intervening trenches being empty, in a few minutes found themselves in the dummy trenches where a like fate to which had overtaken their comrades waited them. It was in fact full of their dead bodies. They in their turn, after suffering grievous losses, were forced to retire, but they did not return to their original trench. The second intervening trench afforded them cover, and in this they stuck, and no efforts of the Turks were sufficient to dislodge them, but it was but a sorry remnant of a fine Battalion. This position was consolidated and here they remained until relieved. So far as is known, no further advance was ever made nor indeed does it seem possible. All efforts to succour the wounded or collect the dead proved fruitless. A few that tried it were killed, and definite orders had to be issued that no further attempts should be made. It was a death-zone where none dared to enter, either Briton or Turk. It is evident that no prisoners could have been taken, and it is practically certain that all men missing that day who did not report themselves afterwards were lost. The account of this most unfortunate affair was given by Lieut. Mellor, who was absent at the time of its occurring, but rejoining the Battalion a few days later heard all there was to be known first-hand.

(Signed) C.W.E. Duncombe
Colonel[23]

For whatever reason, the account provided by Mellor/Duncombe is different from the facts stated in the official War Diaries. Nonetheless, these letters may have alleviated some of the families' concerns.

The remains of William Aitkin, Alexander Cessford, John T. Hardie, George Braidford Johnston and Robert Dickson Young were never recovered. Their names, together with the names of the 20,956 men who died during the Gallipoli campaign but have no known graves, are remembered at the Helles Memorial in Turkey.

Earlston's connection with Gallipoli did not end in July 1915. In August that year, a landing took place at Suvla Bay. An unknown Earlstonian who took part described his experiences in a letter to his former teacher in Earlston:

You will be surprised when you read these few lines which are not written from imagination, but give a short description of the landing at Suvla Bay. We left on 6 August surrounded on all sides by troopships, tugs, lighters, battleships, torpedo boats, and all sorts of craft that are required for such an expedition as we set out to perform. When we were about halfway we heard the boom of the big guns, and as it was the first time we heard them (we could even see the flashes) I, like many others, got so excited that sleep was out of the question, although we had comfortable bunks to go to. When we got to Suvla we found two battleships there before us, and they were giving the Turks something to go on with. But it was nothing to what they got a few hours later when the Divisions got at them. It was now getting light, and the enemy were answering the fire from the ships, many a transport was damaged. The flagship signalled the order 'All men to load rifles and stand to ready for disembarking.' By then two lighters were swarming round the troopships and not a sound was heard as the men and officers quickly got into them, and made for the shore. The Royal Irish Fusiliers landed with a battalion of the Manchester first, and we watched them charge the first ridge (Lala Baba) with the bayonet. What a stirring sight! And the sound of the guns was completely drowned by the cheers that came from the cruisers and the troopships as they reached the top. The Inniskilling Fusiliers were next, and we the Supply Section ASC went on the same lighter. When we neared the shore bullets were hitting the lighter, but no damage was done, as we were all below, and the lighter had a large screen of steel all round to protect the crew. I landed along with the Lieut. and Quartermaster of the Inniskillings, and he was asking about rations when we would make an issue (his first thoughts were for his men), when he was knocked down by shrapnel. We tied up his wound, which was in the shoulder, but afterwards I heard that he had died on the hospital ship. Many a hundred fell in that charge, which for the time being had come to a standstill, as the Turks were making a desperate attempt to cut through, but they broke their line in the centre and our boys charged again, this time gaining a footing on Chocolate Hill, where they entrenched themselves, and there were many wounded who had stuck it and had a rest after their first battle like heroes. I could write page after page, but I'm afraid I am wearying you as no doubt you have read it all in the papers. We have lost our Captain. He was shot crossing the salt lake with a convoy of pack mules with rations, only four men escaping injury; and Lt. Gray, 108 Coy. Had been recommended for the DCM for carrying the Captain into safety under heavy fire. I may say that we were treated very well by our officers, and they would not send us on any errand they thought dangerous. The Captain always went himself. He was a brave man, and we all miss him. We had the best of food, of course the ASC always have, and cigarettes more than we could smoke, thanks to our well-wishers at home.[24]

Enemy fire was not the only cause of death in Gallipoli. The climate was unforgiving with high day-time, thirst-inducing temperatures and bone-chilling temperatures at night. Supplying the men with food and water was difficult, due to the nature of the terrain and the constant threat of sniper fire. Sanitation was also difficult for the same reasons. It was not always possible to recover the bodies and body parts from No Man's Land. Disease became a significant issue.

William Kerr (or 'James', since he seemed to have had a preference for that name) was a worker at the Simpson and Fairbairn tweed mill. He lived with his parents, James and Rachel Kerr, at Green View, a house overlooking the East Green, which was the old horse market. William had a brother, Thomas, who also served in the army. His other siblings were Jane, Euphemia, Helen and Mary.

In May 1915, the 4th Battalion was called up, and William and his fellow villager Louis Fisher sailed for the Dardanelles on 20 May 1915, as part of the Mediterranean Expeditionary Force.

William survived the attack on Achi Baba Nullah and the other enemy actions involving the 4th Battalion unscathed. However, in September 1915, he reported sick. Initially, he was treated at a field hospital in Gallipoli, but as his condition deteriorated, he was transferred to Egypt on board the hospital ship *Karapara*.

He was admitted to the 17th General Hospital in Alexandria on 30 September, where he was diagnosed as suffering from dysentery. His hospital notes record his condition as 'dangerously ill'.

William succumbed to the disease and died on 19 October 1915, aged 29. He is buried in the Alexandria (Chatby) Military and War Memorial cemetery.

A few months later the remnants of the 4th Battalion were evacuated from Gallipoli: 80 men left on the night of 2/3 January 1916, and the remaining 147 men departed on the night of 7/8 January.

The Gallipoli campaign lasted approximately 280 days. The Allies suffered 44,150 fatalities (Great Britain and Ireland 21,255; Australia 8,709; France 10,000; New Zealand 2,779; India 1,358; Newfoundland 49).

The Ottoman Empire recorded 86,692 deaths.

In Great Britain, the Gallipoli campaign was regarded as an example of poor leadership, of 'lions led by donkeys'. In Australia and New Zealand, the number of casualties had a significant impact, since this was the first time these countries had suffered such massive losses. ANZAC (Australia and New Zealand Army Corps) Day, the national Day of Remembrance in Australia and New Zealand, is held on 25 April – the day of the landings in Gallipoli – to remember those 'Who served and died in all wars, conflicts, and peacekeeping operations', and 'the contribution and suffering of all those who have served'.

Chapter 4

1916

In 1892, 23-year-old William Wilkie married Alison Hunter at her parents' house, Leader Vale Lodge, Earlston. Their daughter, Margaret, was born the following year.

William was employed as a stake warper at the tweed mill in the village. In the winter months, he joined other members of the Curling Club to play on one of the village's curling ponds, but his real passion was gardening. He was a member of the Earlston Horticultural Society and held various positions as an elected office-bearer. In 1901, William's life took a significant change. He and his family moved to a house on the High Street and William joined the Yearly Benefit Society as an assurance agent. The venture would last less than ten years since, by 1910, he had returned to his warper job at the tweed mill.

In 1902, William became something of a local celebrity. Lady Binning was driving through the village in a two-wheeled hooded gig towards her home at Mellerstain House. As the gig passed Kilnknowe, the horse began to buck and rear. Lady Binning and her male companion were thrown from the gig and the horse, with gig in tow, took off at a gallop. The gig struck a pile of stones, smashing the shafts and breaking the traces. William, who had seen the accident, gave chase on his bicycle. He eventually caught up with the horse which was lying in a ditch with the reins wrapped around its legs. Fittingly, the horse was found at 'Racecourse Plantation', site of Earlston's long-forgotten racecourse. The horse was untangled and, found to have no cuts or bruises, was led, albeit very lame, to its stable at Mellerstain.

William joined the Earlston Territorial Force, and by 1908 had been promoted to Sergeant. He, along with Colour Sergeant John Burrell, acted as MCs at the Territorial Ball that year. John's wife, Alison, was in charge of the catering and the evening was considered a great success.

In 1915, William was a guard of honour at John Archibald's funeral, but later that year he developed Bright's Disease, a condition that affects the kidneys. William died at home on 10 January 1916, and he is buried in Earlston Parish Church cemetery. His plot is part of the Commonwealth War Graves Commission Cemetery (Figure 12).

Figure 12. Grave of William Wilkie in Earlston churchyard.

The British army was, traditionally, against using conscripts as, it was argued, they lacked *esprit de corps*. D Company of the 4th KOSB consisted almost exclusively of men from Earlston and had a long history, having been established in 1863 as the 'Earlston Rifle Volunteers', under the command of Captain Mitchell, a veteran of the Crimean War. The Volunteers served in the Boer War then, in 1908, they merged with other volunteer forces to form the Territorial Force. However, Earlstonians had *esprit de corps* originating from two old marriage customs.

Tom Murdison, plumber, poet and Earlston worthy, tells it best in an article that was published in 1932:

> An old custom, which has been in vogue from time immemorial, still persists in the old Border town of Earlston – once Ercildoune – famous as the birthplace of Thomas the Rhymer, Scotland's earliest poet and prophet where the ivy clad ruin, Rhymer's Tower, still stands on the side of Leader's glamour-haunted stream after defying the shine and showers of seven long centuries. Earlston was likewise renowned in past days for the hand loom manufacture of gingham, a finely-woven dress fabric which was sold at home and exported all over the world a century ago and more.
>
> After every marriage in the village, coppers are thrown from the house where the marriage take place, and where numerous boys and girls congregate and cry 'Bawbees!' Until the 'scatter' is completed. After this unique part of the ceremony is over the 'best' man, who provides a football, kicks it out to the young men of the town, who, on many occasions, play football up and down the main street hour after hour, without let or hindrance, or even any order or rule in the game. There is no referee and no whistle; no 'feet

up' scrum regulations and no 'free kicks granted to disturb the 'harmony' of the players, or to interrupt their constant, strenuous efforts on the unmeasured hard street pitch – a game on these happy occasions, without even a time limit. All play like 'Springboks' let loose for the evening. The marriage game of football has altered greatly since I took part in it during my young days. The custom then was that all the natives born east of the present Post Office, in the High Street, Earlston, kicked the ball to the east end, and those born west of that dividing line kicked it to the west end, as members of each section were determined to keep the ball in their own 'town-end' or territory. No matter how friendly boys and young men when participating against each other in various games, great rivalry existed among them while kicking a marriage ball on the street. If one of either side got the ball and tried to run east or west with it in his arms he was severely tackled and pulled down on the hard road, or thrown without mercy against the wall of a home, so that few tried to carry the ball and run with it in those days, owing to the danger of hard knocks.

On ba' nights, many house windows have been broken, but the difficulty was always overcome by public subscription which was freely given to replace broken glass. I can remember when large round rubber balls were thrown out after each marriage, similar to the ordinary rubber balls girls play with at school nowadays. Some of these balls were seven and eight inches in diameter and quite thick. If the ball burst, as it sometimes did, by hard kicking, the game of course came to an end. About 1877, when Earlston Rugby

Football Club was started, an ordinary rugby rubber and leather ball was introduced. It was decorated with red, white and blue silk ribbons and since then, the rugby ball has always been used, with the exception of a few years when Earlston could boast an Association team, and a round Association ball was kicked. An old native told me in my boyhood that pigs' bladders covered with a coarse fabric were used prior to the days of rubber and leather footballs. Whenever pigs were killed in the parish, the bladders were saved for forthcoming marriages, and covered and preserved by members of the family related to the bride, and thrown out immediately after the happy event took place.[25]

At the end of the match, the ball was given to the school children so that they could be part of the tradition by playing with the ball in the school playground. This inclusiveness and the memories that the games left, ensured *esprit de corps* among the folk of the village.

Such was the casualty rate in Flanders, France and Gallipoli that the regular army, even with its numbers swollen by volunteers, was all but annihilated. For the military Chiefs of Staff and the Government a way had to be found to increase manpower to the military.

So it was, in January 1916, that the British Government introduced the Military Service Act, which mandated conscription for military service for all men aged between 18 and 40. Widowers with children and ministers of religion were exempt. The Act also established Military Service Tribunals, which adjudicated claims for exemptions from military service.

For Earlston residents, any claims for exemptions were heard by the Military Tribunal, which convened in Duns, the county town for Berwickshire.

A Village at War

The tribunal was presided over by Sheriff Macaulay-Smith, assisted by a clerk and six tribunal members drawn from residents. There was a member of the army, who acted as a military advisor, and a military clerk assisted him.

Some of the pleas appear frivolous. For example, the farmer at Belville, Coldstream, sought an exemption for his ploughman, Michael Denham, 18. The employer said he had no suitable accommodation for taking on a substitute, and did not want a stranger. The military representative advisor responded: 'You would have had to take strangers had you been in the south of England, where men are billeted on families'.

Sheriff Macaulay-Smith asked, 'How would you like to get into the trenches yourself?'

The employer replied, 'I would just have to do it.'

The Sheriff replied, 'Quite so.'

And with that, the exemption was refused, and Michael Denham was sent to fight for King and Country.[26]

In another case, Lady Reay of Carolside claimed that her forester should be exempt because his work involved the manufacture of fence posts which were used to support the barbed-wire trench defences. The tribunal pointed out that metal stakes support the barbed wire, and in any event, the output of one man was a 'bagatelle' in the grand scheme of things. The case was dismissed.[27]

The findings of each claim could mean the difference between life or death for the applicant.

In one case a farmer pleading on behalf of his two sons was asked by the military representative, 'Don't you think that it is the duty of every man who has two sons to contribute one'.

Sheriff Macaulay-Smith then asked. 'Which of these sons would be most easily spared?'[28]

No doubt the Sheriff was referring to being spared from work, but with the slaughter in Flanders and France, he could equally have been referring to the sons' lives.

Another case involved ploughmen from Fans, a farm on the outskirts of Earlston. Mr Herbertson, the farmer, claimed an exemption for five of his ploughmen, which included two brothers, Joseph and David Borthwick. The brothers belonged to a large family headed by Thomas Borthwick and his wife Janet (née Swinton). By 1916, the husband and wife were no longer able to work – he was 74 and she was 65 – and therefore relied on family for support. The eldest son, Thomas, had married Agnes Oliver in 1892, and of their five sons, three had left home. Similarly, the three daughters had left the family home. Thus, the two youngest sons, Joseph, 25, and David, 24, were the only remaining offspring to care for their elderly parents. The *Berwick Advertiser* covered their case as follows:

> David Borthwick, who was present in Court, was asked if he were quite anxious to serve, and his answer was 'If I were fit'. The Sheriff asked him if his brother Joseph had any medical defects, and David's answer was 'Well, he once went through an operation.' Joseph explained to the Bench that 'he did not feel very strong in the back since he went through this operation'. Tribunal member Mr Campbell Renton asked 'You are quite willing to serve the country if you can get past that doctor?' Applicant – 'I have got my father and mother to keep.'[29]

The tribunal decided that David's claim should be refused and that Joseph should be exempt till 28 May.

It has not been possible to establish what the outcome was in the follow-up to Joseph's case. He may have been given a permanent exemption; he may have been rejected on medical grounds by the military when he enlisted; or he may have served and survived. What is known is that, in 1923, he married Elspeth Graham Strachan in Edinburgh, and died in Portobello in 1973, aged 81.

For David, the die was cast, and like his brother, he would not reach old age.

The war effort was having a severe impact on manufacturing industries and agriculture. At a time when there needed to be an increase in manufacturing output, military service was stripping the factories of their male workforce. The German U-boats were sinking ships bringing food supplies to Great Britain, putting pressure on farms to increase their yields. Agriculture was suffering from the shortage of skilled ploughmen and heavy horses, which had been requisitioned by the army to pull artillery pieces rather than ploughs.

A frequent reason for employers seeking exemptions for their workers was that there were no male workers available. In response, the War Office published *Women's War Work*.[30] The book was a guide for tribunals, listing almost every job in a range of occupations in which women were successfully employed, therefore the tribunal could rule on the validity for an exemption. Agriculture was treated somewhat differently, and the occupation was listed, together with particulars of the occupation and remarks. For example, for the occupation 'Agricultural Labourer–Farm Servant', the particulars of the occupation were given as: 'Bondagers; datal (sic) man (on farm); drill man; hay and straw binder; hedger and ditcher; hop ground labourer; mulcher; strapper; twitcher.' The corresponding remarks were: 'Large numbers of women are doing the different kinds of work mentioned, and are being increasingly useful.'

The book noted that, 'Wives have taken up their husbands' work, sisters their brothers', daughters their fathers', even mother their sons'.' However, regardless of whether a woman could do the work, the recent census for Earlston showed that most women folk worked anyway. Those who didn't were bringing up young families and since there was no Welfare State, people worked well into their sixties and seventies, meaning that leaving children with grandparents was not always an option.

Sometimes the efforts of women were refused.

Elsie Inglis was by any measure an extraordinary woman blessed with determination, foresight and a passion for women's rights. She was one of the earliest medical doctors, having qualified as a doctor at Edinburgh University. Dr Inglis set up her practice in the city, performed surgical work at the Edinburgh Hospital for Women and Children and opened a hospital on the High Street for maternity cases. Additionally, she was a suffragette who campaigned for women's rights. In 1914, Dr Inglis anticipated the need for more military hospitals. She approached the military authorities with the idea that the Scottish Suffrage Society would fund a hospital that would be staffed entirely by women. The authorities told her: 'My good lady, go home and sit still.'

Fortunately for thousands of soldiers, Dr Inglis was not minded to go home and sit still. She turned initially to the Red Cross, then to the Serbian and French authorities, who were grateful to receive her assistance. By December 1914, she had established hospitals in France, Serbia, Corsica, Greece and Romania. In all, fourteen hospitals were created that served the Allies – except the British.

Dr Inglis was taken prisoner in Serbia, released and made her way to Russia, but had to evacuate to Great Britain in 1917, following the Russian Revolution. She arrived in Newcastle in November, but was too ill to travel onwards and died the next day.

The work of Dr Inglis caught the public imagination. Spokespersons would visit towns and cities to explain the work of the organization and take the opportunity to ask for donations. In August, during a visit to Earlston, a presentation made to the workers of the tweed mill raised £3 18s 6d, and during the same visit the children of the Earlston Public School handed over £3 7s raised from jars and bottles they had collected.

Like Henry Forbes, David Paterson was another Earlston man who had emigrated to Canada. He was born in Earlston on

10 May 1891, to Stewart Paterson, a mole- and rabbit-catcher, and his wife, Jane. David was employed as a farm labourer until 1907, when he decided to emigrate. David sailed from Glasgow onboard SS *Numidian* and arrived in Montreal on 27 June 1907. Once in Canada, he became a carpenter, most likely in Saskatchewan, until moving to Halifax, Nova Scotia, where he enlisted on 25 August 1915. He had previous military experience having served five years in the 4th Battalion King's Own Scottish Borderers (Territorials) when he was in Scotland, then one month in the 22nd Saskatchewan Light Horse before enlisting in the Royal Canadian Regiment. His previous experience stood him in good stead as he was promoted to Lance Corporal on 7 October 1915. Three weeks later David and his regiment were shipped to Europe, disembarking in Boulogne on 1 November 1915.

The Royal Canadian Regiment took part in the Somme campaign; a campaign that, in just four months, inflicted around 620,000 Allied and 500,000 Germans casualties.

David was killed by enemy machine-gun fire on 3 August 1916. He was 25 years old. He is buried in Menin Road South Military Cemetery.

It wasn't just the men at the front who were at risk from enemy action. German Zeppelins had bombed coastal towns, even though blackout conditions had existed along the coast since August 1914. In their search for new targets, airships started to search inland, so that by February 1916, the Government introduced the Lighting Regulations, enforcing blackouts of buildings, streets and vehicles nationwide. In Earlston, notices were posted throughout the village instructing residents to darken business premises and homes at night, to confuse the German aircrews.

However, there was a genuine concern that the Lighting Regulations (or Order) probably caused more casualties than the

Zeppelin raids. This was blamed on too literal an interpretation of the law. An editorial in the *Southern Reporter* noted that:

> The Order never intended that in populous places and twisting and dangerous thoroughfares there should be absolute mirk, or, at the other extreme, that there should glaring patches light showing up particular points. Properly to follow the regulations requires common-sense on the part of the public and of the authorities, for both may be liable to run extremes. The regulations are apparently to provide against bright lights, not to insist upon the darkness which so widely prevails. In Selkirk, we have the two extremes. The thoroughfares are pitch dark, and at certain military billets, there are big patches of light. We hope it will not be long till the happy medium is struck, which shall make the journeyings of persons who have to go about town after dark tolerably safe. [31]

In April, the *Southern Reporter* carried the following article:

HEAVY FINES FOR FAILING TO OBSCURE LIGHTS.

> At Jedburgh, on Thursday, Sheriff Baillie imposed the following fines for infringements of Lighting Order No. 1 by failing obscure lights David Cockburn, manufacturer, Jedburgh, £15, or 21 days; M. C. Noble, licensed grocer, Jedburgh, and Mrs Noble, £7 10s each, ten days; George Steel Forbes, hotel keeper, Jedburgh Arms Hotel, £10, 10 days; George Beveridge grocer, Kelso. £7 10s, or seven days.[32]

A few weeks later the *Western Daily Press* reported that at Brackley police court, Lady Margaret Smith, wife of the Attorney General, had been fined £1 for having unshaded lights at her house. Naturally, there was an outcry at the injustice of levels of fines imposed for what was in effect the same crime.

Things came to a head in August when, in the House of Commons, Sir John Jardine, MP for Roxburgh, asked the Secretary for Scotland, about the trial and conviction of Jedburgh man Mr David Cockburn before Sheriff Substitute Baillie; the fine of £15 imposed for an infraction of the Lighting Order for failing to obscure sufficiently the light in his premises; whether any previous conviction or malice or atrocity or connivance with the enemy was charged, proved or admitted; and whether the learned judge found any specific act to be a reason for the amount of the fine inflicted.

In reply, the Secretary for Scotland (Mr Tennant) stated that: 'I would refer my honourable friend to the statement made by my right honourable and learned friend the Lord Advocate in the Debate on Scottish Estimates yesterday in this House.'[33]

The debate rumbled on without reaching a satisfactory conclusion. Meantime the law continued to be applied inconsistently. For example, in the Justice of the Peace Court in Lauder, Provost Lindsay and Baillie Robertson heard the case brought against William Baillie, farm servant, of Midburn, Matthew Douglas, a groom, of Whitehall, John Robson and George P. Brown of Longeroft, for cycling without lights after lighting-up time. Each was fined 2s 6d.[34] Then another case was heard in which a man stood accused of having too bright a light on his bicycle. James Bain, a farm servant from New Smailholm, pleaded guilty in Duns Sheriff Court to having, 'On Saturday, 6 September, at 9.45 a.m. in Market Place, Earlston, ridden a bicycle without having the front glass of the lamp properly obscured'. Sheriff Macaulay-Smith imposed a fine of 10s-, or five days' imprisonment.[35]

Deaths caused by blackout conditions did occur, however. In November a young boy from St Abbs, a Berwickshire fishing village, drowned. Alexander Dickson, a 7-year-old schoolboy, lived with his grandparents at Harbour Terrace in the town. As was his custom, Alexander delivered the evening paper to a neighbour's house. The houses are very close to the harbour's edge and, because of the blackout, it was very dark at the time. The neighbour raised the alarm when Alexander failed to show. A flashlight was shone on the dark water of the harbour, revealing the evening paper floating on the surface. A few minutes later, Alexander's lifeless body was recovered from the sea.[36]

In August, several of Earlston's recruits were home on leave from basic training at Catterick Camp, in Yorkshire. Bill Frater, who had joined the Royal Scots (Dandy Ninth), was in the village, as was Henry Simpson, who was a member of the Queen's Edinburgh Rifles. Three men from the King's Own Scottish Borderers – George Nicol, Robert Brown and David Ballantyne – were enjoying their leave before their departure to the front.

David Ballantyne was a private in the 7/8th (Service) Battalion of the KOSB, and destined to fight on the fields of the Somme. Little did David know, but this was his last month alive. The British military had mounted a campaign in the Somme region of France starting on 1 July 1916, and ending later that year in November. When David arrived in France in late August, his battalion was part of the 46th Brigade, which was in turn part of the 15th (Scottish) Division.

Military planners had decided to capture the town of Martinpuich and the 15th Division was selected to accomplish the task.

On 12 September, David's battalion was digging trenches in advance of the assault on enemy lines. Parties of men, 25 strong, left the British positions to prepare the ground, working under cover of darkness and the British bombardment of the German lines, which did not cease for another five days.

In the late afternoon of 14 September, David and his comrades made their way to their allotted positions. Each man carried two sandbags, a pick or shovel and either red flares or smoke bombs, the latter to clear enemy dugouts. At 4.00 a.m. the following day, hot tea was served before the assault. By 6.45 a.m. the first objective had been achieved with comparatively few casualties. However, as the men fought to reach the second objective, they overran the creeping barrage of the British artillery. They were now exposed to both British and German artillery, as well as German machine-gun fire. The casualty numbers began to mount, and by the end of the day, 1,854 men had been killed or wounded.

A month after the engagement, David's parents, Robert and Isabella Ballantyne, received official word that David was reported as missing. As the *Berwickshire News and General Advertiser* reported on 17 October 1916: 'Pte David Ballantyne, K.O.S.B. is officially reported missing. He entered the trenches somewhere in France on 13 September, was in action on 15th, and has been missing since. He belongs to Earlston, his father being in employment at Haughhead.'[37]

On 12 December the newspaper reported that, 'No further information has come to hand regarding Pte. David Ballantyne, reported missing last month.'[38]

It was not until over a year after David had gone into action that his parents received the news they had been dreading: David was now considered 'killed in action'. A notice appeared in the *Berwickshire News and General Advertiser* in September 1917.

In Memoriam

In loving memory of Pte. David Ballantyne, dearly loved and only son of Mr and Mrs Ballantyne, Thorn Street, Earlston, reported missing 15 September 1916, now reported killed, aged 19.

> We think we see his smiling face.
> As bade his last, goodbye;
> And left his home for ever
> In a foreign land to die;
> But the hardest part is yet to come
> When the warriors all return.
> And we miss amidst the cheering crowds
> The face one loved.
>
> (Ever remembered by his sorrowing Father, Mother, and Sister.)[39]

If a soldier was killed or reported missing in action, the Army Council's guideline was that since a soldier was only entitled to pay while he was alive, his pay should be stopped immediately. If he were reported missing in action, relatives would be informed, but then there were weeks when an investigation was conducted, to establish if the missing man was dead and, if so, the date of his death. Where a soldier was reported missing, he was assumed to have died if he had not been heard of for four weeks after his next of kin had been notified.

Once the soldier's date of death had been established, any money credited to his account beyond that date would be recredited to the public purse. A man's pay that had been credited to his account would then be disbursed following his will – something that all service personnel were required to make.

In David's case, the Soldier's Effects Register shows that he had £2 15s in cash, which was paid to the family in July 1917. Additionally, a war gratuity payment of £9 was paid in July 1919. His Dependent's Pension record card shows that a weekly pension of 4 shillings was paid to his mother, starting on 7 August 1917. The record card was updated in May 1935 following Isabella's death, recording the change of beneficiary to David's father, Robert.

In the post-war years, when parents of dead soldiers were asked about their sons, there could be no words to describe the loss of a child or, in David's case, the anguish of waiting over a year to have their worst fears confirmed. And somehow a war gratuity of £9 does not seem to repay the loss of a brave son who had to advance on enemy positions, under fire, armed with two sandbags and a shovel.

Henry Cunningham Turnbull was eight years younger than his brother William Turnbull, and like his brother, had enlisted in King's Own Scottish Borderers. During the attack on Achi Baba, he was wounded, taken prisoner by the Turks and held in Bilemedik Pouzanti then Kiangri camps.

The Turks allowed prisoners to write postcards to their families, and Henry had written home at every opportunity. His messages were generally cheery and insisted that he was in good health.

The war against the Turkish Ottoman army had spread to Mesopotamia, modern-day Iraq, where the British deployed the Mesopotamia Expeditionary Force. The 6th Poona Division, part of the Expeditionary Force, was besieged at a place called Kut-al-Amara, between December 1915 and April 1916. The Division surrendered on 29 April 1916, resulting in thousands of British and Indian troops being captured. The British Government tried to buy their release with an initial offer of £1,000,000, which was rejected, as was a second offer of £2,000,000. Instead, an agreement was reached, allowing 13,672 British and Indian prisoners and 1,136 sick and wounded held by the Turks to be exchanged for Ottoman prisoners held by the British.

To transport the prisoners by boat to Baghdad, the Turks requested 1,000 tons of coal from the British, but the British commander based in southern Iraq refused. Consequently, so that the exchange could proceed, the Ottoman army marched the men overland, some 170 kilometres.

Of the 2,680 British 'other ranks' prisoners, 1,306 died either during the march or at their destination. Henry was most likely one of these men and so is remembered at the Baghdad (North Gate) War Cemetery.

Henry's last postcard home was dated 24 September and arrived in Earlston on 10 October, together with a postcard from a fellow prisoner, a Sergeant Wood from Stow. Sergeant Wood's message was that he had heard that Henry had died, although it would be some time before the official word was received confirming Henry's death.

Henry's father died in 1925 aged 70 and is buried in Earlston churchyard. His gravestone commemorates both of his sons, William and Henry (Figure 13).

Figure 13. Family grave in Earlston churchyard commemorating William and Henry Turnbull.

Chapter 5

1917

In early January the people of Earlston woke to the news that Lord Binning, eldest son of the Earl of Haddington, had died. He had been on a brief leave at his father's East Lothian seat at Tyninghame and suffering from a chill, which progressed into pneumonia. He died on 12 January.

Newspapers, both national and provincial, carried obituaries mentioning his military career in the Royal Horse Guards. Some referenced his command of the Lothians and Borders Horse, the regiment that he was most closely associated with by the people of Earlston.

The region was suffering from severe weather, with 14 January was reckoned to be the worst day for snowstorms and snowdrifts for over two years. Farmers reported that, due to the weather and manpower shortages, work in the fields was about a month behind where it should have been. Agriculture was of such significance to Earlston that any external influence on farming, such as weather or Government policy, affected villagers.

In 1915, the Government had recognized the importance of food security and launched a food production campaign, with a focus on encouraging increased production of grain and potatoes. By 1917, the situation became critical, forcing the Government to take powers to provide help to agriculture. County War Agriculture Committees were established to publicize and implement Government aims and identify local shortages of labour, horses, machinery and supplies.

However, the aims of the Board of Agriculture were at odds with those of the War Office. The situation was causing such consternation that an editorial in the *Berwickshire Advertiser* challenged the Government leadership on the conflict between the two bodies:

> The decision of the President the English Board of Agriculture to call up one-half of those men engaged in farm labour whom the Tribunals have refused certificates of exemption is certain to cause much uneasiness and inconvenience at a time singularly ill-suited for such order. It is evident that the War Office has been pressing the new President (Clarence Prothero) for more men, else the summary command would not have gone forth at a moment when the nation was seriously led to believe that the future supply of food was a problem which must be regarded in a serious light. To the men taken several thousands of Class C3 men (Note: Class C3 men were those born after 1895) are to be placed at the disposal farmers, and while it is admitted that hardship will ensue, it is hoped that they will do their utmost to carry on in the exceptional and difficult circumstances. After all the recent outbursts about ploughing uncultivated land, the decision to remove some 20,000–30,000 dependable tillage labourers appears very incongruous. It would seem that the

demands of the War Office are as powerful now they have been at any previous time and that Mr Prothero has no other alternative than yield implicit obedience, the same as was done by his immediate predecessor, Lord Crawford. It is difficult, if not impossible, reconcile taking the remaining fit men off the land with the great efforts which have within the last few weeks been made to conserve and increase our home food supplies. It makes one rub their eyes and ask if it is really true that the problem is a serious one. It is only lately that Prothero himself likened the home situation to that of a besieged city. The decline of ten per cent in our wheat acreage last year was entirely due to the want labour, for the farmers had special inducements for prices to cultivate this crop. The class of men who are to take the places of the workers now called up are ill-qualified, of poor physique and training to step into the breach, and how farmers are to carry on and increase food supplies under such untoward circumstances it impossible understand. It is true that the War Authorities must have the men to win the war, but the men now removed from the land are no less indispensable to nation's safety than those who fight as soldiers. It has been pointed out that the solution to the difficulty would have been to have raised the age limit to 45. The four additional years would have given us more men than are needed. France and Germany take men 48; Austria-Hungary men up 50. But certainly the very conflicting claims the army and agriculture are each so strong and equally important that is impossible see how even the new Government can accomplish miracles unless it takes bold and practical steps to achieve this, and certainly, the country was looking it for a lead in anything that would tend to better organization for the more effectual prosecution of the war.[40]

This piece was powerful and, for its time, controversial. Under the Defence of the Realm Act of 1914, it was prohibited for any newspaper to publish reports or statements that were liable to undermine loyalty to the King, recruitment or confidence in the country. And this was no idle threat. In 1916 alone the Government had scrutinized 38,000 literary articles, 25,000 photographs and 300,000 private telegrams.

Meanwhile, in Earlston, villagers heard that the Duns Military Tribunal, held in January 1917, had announced that it was withdrawing the certificates of exemption for twenty-seven men, aged between 26 and 40. All the men were employed in agriculture.

It wasn't just food production that was an issue. Food distribution was of equal importance. In November, the Berwickshire Food Control and Economy Committee met to address the distribution issue, and a transport subcommittee was created with members of Food Economy Committee and representative tradesmen.

The chairman tabled a document that he called *Suggested Rules for the Guidance of a Transport Committee,* which were:

1. That tradesmen should only serve customers within a limited area, and that such an area to be decided by the Committee;
2. That grocers should serve the same round more than once in every 14 days;
3. That motor vans should be limited to an average mileage not to exceed 130 miles in a week (or three days in a week);

> 4. That tradesmen be permitted to buy a horse for the purpose of transport without the sanction of the Food Control Committee.

Earlston had, at that time, two bakers (Aitchison and the Earlston Co-op), four grocers (Weatherston, Dodds, Taylor and Smith) and two butchers (Walter Donaldson and Mrs Miles). Each were affected by the guidelines.

After considerable debate, Guideline 1 was rejected, but only by a majority of one vote, whereas 12 votes to 2 resulted in Guideline 2 being adopted.

The committee then undertook to write a letter to the village ministers and school headmaster outlining its aims. For ministers, the letter stated that:

> It is the hope of the Food Control and Economy Committee that every Minister of Religion in the County will on the first Sabbath of December, especially direct the attention of his congregation, in whatever seems best to him, to this vital matter.

But for food control and economy, the situation would continue to deteriorate until, in 1918, food rationing had to be introduced.

Knitting and sewing and other fundraising activities allowed many of the women to contribute to the war effort. In February, the Earlston Orchestra, under the leadership of Samuel Fisher, entertained the 'moss pickers' to a musical programme.

The moss pickers were mainly women from the War Relief Guild, who picked, cleaned and dried sphagnum moss. In 1916, the women had collected over 1,500 lbs (680 kgs) of moss, which was used for wound dressings.

Early in the war, it was recognized that an alternative to the traditional cotton wound dressing had to be found. Cotton was in short supply and therefore, unable to keep up with the demand of around 50 million bandages needed each year. The solution lay in sphagnum moss, an ancient wound-dressing material, which was known to be highly absorbent, mildly antiseptic due to its iodine content, and also acted as a deodorant. Gathering the plentiful supply of moss around Earlston provided women with another way to contribute to the war effort.

Henry Elliott was born in Roxburghshire, and like his father Robert, was a farm steward (or farm manager). Brought up on farms in Roxburghshire, Henry was living at Crossflat Farm near St Boswells, when he married Catherine Paxton in 1910. A year later their daughter Margaret was born. Henry moved from farm to farm wherever there was work, while Catherine made the family home at Acre Cottage in Earlston.

Sometime later, Henry moved to a farm near Hawick, where he enlisted in the 7/8th Service Battalion of the King's Own Scottish Borderers.

In Flanders in late February, the Middlesex Regiment carried out a raid on German trenches, capturing twenty-six prisoners. Naturally, the Germans retaliated and sent a barrage of shells towards the British positions. A communication trench nicknamed 'Islington Street' seemed to be the target. Communication trenches were vital because they allowed men and equipment to access the forward trenches. Henry and other men from the service battalion were ordered to keep the trench clear despite the incoming shells.

The battalion sustained many casualties including Henry, who died the following day from the wounds he had received.

On 9 March 1917, ten days after Henry's death, the *Jedburgh Gazette* reported:

> Mrs Elliot, Acre Cottage, West End, Earlston (formerly 2 Exchange Street, Jedburgh), has received official intimation of the death in France of her husband, Private Henry Elliot, KOSB. He was seriously wounded in action on 26 February and died on the 27th. He had been on service for over two years. Previous to enlisting he was farm steward at Flex, Hawick. Besides the widow, there are two children left.

For parents to lose a child must be devastating, but to lose two is almost beyond comprehension. And yet that is the fate that befell the Hardies, the Turnbulls and the Youngs.

Robert Young, Archibald and Margaret Young's second eldest, had fought in the South-Africa War, returned to hero's welcome only to re-enlist and be killed at Gallipoli. George, their eldest son, had continued to work in the family's boot-making business.

In 1916, George married Agnes Kerr in Hawick (although both were living in Earlston). The number of marriages registered in the village during the war remained relatively constant compared with the pre- and post-war years, but George and Agnes' marriage was noteworthy.

A minister performed most marriages in Scotland after the banns had been read in church for three consecutive Sundays. For a couple wanting to get married where the groom-to-be was only home on leave for a short time, the three weeks to read the banns could be a problem.

However, in Scotland, there was a solution: a couple could be wed by an 'irregular' marriage, in which the bride and groom made a declaration in front of witnesses. By showing 'proofs' of their marriage to a Sheriff or a Sheriff Substitute, a warrant could be obtained, allowing the wedding to be registered by the local registrar. The church frowned on the practice, considering it an encouragement to 'live in sin', but it was nonetheless legal up until 1940.

On 22 May 1916, at Oliver Place in Hawick, and in front of witnesses Abraham Walter Kerr, a tailor living in Hawick, and Andrew Renwick, a draper and also a Hawick resident, George and his bride Agnes Kerr were married by declaration and, having received a warrant from the Sheriff Substitute of Roxburghshire, the Hawick registrar registered their marriage.

George enlisted in the King's Own Scottish Borderers although he was later transferred to the Highland Light Infantry. His battalion was one of many engaged in the Battle of Arras. The battle started on 9 April at 5.30 a.m., and by First-World-War standards the advance was spectacular, with the most distance gained than any previous action. However, this was at a cost. After three days of fighting the 12th Battalion's casualty toll was 244, including 27 killed or missing presumed killed, 7 missing and 210 wounded. George was one of the men who died on 11 April.

On 22 May 1917, the *Berwickshire News and General Advertiser* announced that George was reported missing in action.[41]

The Young family were to suffer another loss. On 18 February 1916, their daughter, Jane Brydon Young, married James Roger, a plumber journeyman from Stirling. James enlisted in the Argyll and Sutherland Highlanders and was killed in action on 9 April 1917.

Within a couple of months of war being declared, Robert White enlisted in the Kings Own Scottish Borderers. He was born at Hendersyde Home Farm in 1894, and by the time he joined up, he was working as a ploughman at Upper Blainslie farm, near Earlston.

After enlisting, Robert went to Galashiels to complete his basic training before being posted in Catterick Garrison. In 1915, he married Isabella Wilson, a worker at the tweed factory in Earlston, and their daughter, Margaret, was born later that year.

In December 1916, he was posted to Egypt, travelling via France. He boarded the troopship SS *Iverina* in Marseilles bound for Alexandria. Robert probably didn't know it, but the SS *Iverina* was under the command of Captain Thomas Turner. The year before Turner had been the captain of the *Lusitania* when it was torpedoed by a German submarine. History was about to repeat itself.

On New Year's Day 1917, en route to Egypt with 2,400 troops on board, the SS *Iverina* was torpedoed by a German submarine: 84 soldiers and 36 crew members drowned. Robert was one of the survivors and his lifeboat was towed to Greece.

Robert eventually made it to Egypt and participated in the Second Battle for Gaza in April 1917. Such was the slaughter that the history of the KOSB notes: 'Two Floddens for the Lowlands of Scotland within the space of two years!' – referring to Gallipoli and Gaza.[42]

Robert was one of the many soldiers posted as missing. It would be over a year before he was officially presumed killed in action, the date of death given as 19 April 1917. His remains were never recovered, and he is commemorated on the Jerusalem Memorial.

In 1919, Robert's wife Isabella married Andrew Anderson and died in 1967, aged 72. Robert's daughter, Margaret, who was only two years old when he died, married John McCormack, a baker from Penpont in Dumfriesshire, in 1934.

Arthur Steedman was the youngest of John and Isabella Steedman's three sons. Arthur was born in Earlston in 1887, when his father was a bank clerk at the Commercial Bank on the High Street. Arthur and his family moved frequently as required by the bank, but the moves resulted in John's promotion and a return to Earlston as the Bank Agent.

Arthur seemed to enjoy the military, although not enough to make it his career. His father had been a captain in the Volunteer Brigade of the King's Own Scottish Borderers and Arthur joined the Lothian and Borders Horse and, in 1908, received the award as the Smartest Trooper of the Year. The award, a silver cup, was presented by Lord Binning, the commanding officer of the regiment. It was noted that Arthur had, 'Made a very promising beginning as a Border cavalryman'.

In 1910, Arthur travelled from Glasgow to Montreal on board the SS *Hesperian*. He seems to have been unsure if this move would be permanent or temporary, electing to travel as a 'tourist' rather than a migrant. He settled in British Columbia then, in 1913, his fiancée, Winifred Theresa Beattie, travelled on the SS *Empress of Britain* to join him. The couple were married in Vernon, British Columbia, on 15 August 1914.

In 1915, Arthur felt compelled to return to Britain to, 'Do his bit for King and Country'. He and his wife travelled to New York, then sailed on the SS *Cameronia*, arriving in Glasgow on 20 October 1915. Arthur's return to Earlston was heralded in the *Southern Reporter*:

> Some time ago Mr Arthur Steedman left British Columbia, where he had been settled for two or three years and returned to this country 'to do his bit' for King and Country. Not long ago his brother, Mr Robert Steedman, left good prospects in Burmah and came home here for the same purpose. He is now a commissioned officer in the HLI. Mr Arthur Steedman, it is now learned, has got a commission in the Scottish Rifles. These patriotic young men are the sons of the late Mr John Steedman, banker, Earlston.[43]

Arthur gained a commission in the 10th Battalion Scottish Rifles and was serving as a lieutenant when his daughter, Jeanette Winifred, was born on 13 May 1916. By this time, Arthur and his family were living in Regents Park Road, London.

On 24 March 1917, Arthur was leading a trench-clearing party. Within the first minute of the action, a British artillery shell fell short, exploding between the British front trench and Arthur and his men. Arthur was severely wounded in the back and died six days later. The 10th Battalion War Diary indicates that this single shell killed two men and injured six others.

Arthur is buried in Duisans British Cemetery, Étrun, France.

In April, the spring holiday was a pretty miserable affair. On the Sunday of the holiday, the shops closed, the banks closed on Friday as well as the Saturday, whereas workers at the tweed mill worked their regular Saturday half-shift. The cold weather and high rail fares meant most people stayed at home.

The traditional hot cross buns were not evident; a fact that was blamed on the regulations controlling the supply of food.

Military tribunals continued to make the news, although in this case in a light-hearted way. At the June meeting a Mr Millar, a solicitor, represented James Archibald, the Earlston baker whose son had died in 1915. At an earlier tribunal, James's other son John had been granted an exemption, but that exemption had been given on the basis that a substitute was found. Mr Millar explained that a replacement had been found, but inexplicably, he had been sent to Ireland instead of Earlston.[44]

At this, the Sheriff responded, 'Quite an excusable mistake. In London, you know, they may not know the difference between Earlston and Ireland.' (Laughter.)

Mr Millar replied, 'Just so. (Laughter). Well, unfortunately, this man who would be an acceptable substitute had been sent to a hospital in Ireland for his arm was wounded by shrapnel. He was now in a convalescent home.'

Mr Archibald stated that, 'He will be suitable, I think. He went through the Gallipoli campaign and is in the substitution class.'

The exemption was extended for another three weeks.

However, the review of exemptions was a serious business. At the Berwick Military Tribunal meeting held in November, the military representative told the tribunal that 235 men had been granted an exemption.[45] The men with exemptions were expected to join an organization such as the Voluntary Aid Detachment or Volunteer Corps. The representative examined two men who had failed to meet this condition. The men were employed as potmen at the Spittal Chemical Works, and they stated that, at the end of their working day, they were so exhausted that they were barely able to walk home. Besides, they claimed, they did the work of four men and that the task was 'arduous in nature'. In response, the representative told the men:

> Do you know that in case of an invasion you men would be sent into the country with the women and children, and men of 55 would be fighting to protect you? You are immensely better off than if we were sending you to France.

They were ordered to become efficient volunteers, or their exemption would be cancelled.

The war effort was starting to take its toll on businesses in the village. In June, the tweed mill announced that it was having to cut back on the number of working hours. However, the mill owners agreed to increase the wages of men by 5 shillings per week, women by 4 shillings and boys and girls by 2 shillings to minimize the hardship the workforce was bound to suffer. This gesture received coverage in the national press.

The same month, at a meeting of the Border Counties Cooperative Conference Association, it was announced that thanks to the donations from other societies, the Earlston branch was now, 'in a position to bring itself in line with the other Societies of the Borders'. Earlston was the first cooperative to be established in Berwickshire, and it had almost ceased trading as a consequence of the war.

A Village at War

The Earlston Auction Mart had not held sales for six weeks, leading to rumours of its impending closure, which would be a blow not only for local butchers, but would also deprive villagers of a source of income. It would be several months before the Mart resumed regular business.

And just as businesses were suffering, so was the social life of the village. Clubs and organizations, whose members were men of military age, were hardest hit. The village rugby and football teams had ceased playing. Clubs with an older membership, such as the village bowling and curling clubs, fared better, as did organizations with women members, such as the village Ladies Golf Club. The Angling Club continued to function with a reduced membership of men who were beyond conscription age. At least the fish caught during competitions were provided to the Craigleith Military Hospital.

Even the village bible class suffered resulting in the minister reporting that: 'This year was numerically affected due to the circumstances of the country demanding the presence of her youth elsewhere than at home to defend her cause in these perilous times'.[46]

Thomas Faichney moved to Earlston in the early 1900s, to take up work as a tweed web drawer at the tweed mill. He'd had the same job when he lived with his widowed mother and his younger brother, James, in Hawick. In Earlston, Thomas lodged with Isabella Wallace and her family, in Kidgate. Thomas remained single and socialized with his workmates and members of the Earlston Rugby Club.

In 1912, he and around twelve of his friends met in the White Swan to celebrate the forthcoming marriage of their friend John Haig. John lived in Arnot Place and was a keen rugby player, as well as a mill worker. At the gathering were William Aitken, William Wilkie and Thomas – three men who would not live through the war.

Sometime before enlisting in the 8/10th Gordon Highlanders, Thomas moved back to Hawick to take up work as a porter at the station. In 1917, Thomas's battalion was engaged in the 3rd Battle of

Ypres. From their camp in the Brandhoek area, the men marched to a forward camp at Verdrenhoek on 20 August, before moving to the front line the following day. The attack was launched at 4.45 a.m. on 22 August, but after advancing only 200 yards, the men were forced to retreat to their original front-line position. Attack after attack was mounted over the next days and nights, until 27 August, when the men were ordered back to Toronto Camp, another forward camp. The battalion had sustained 192 casualties, including 13 missing, of whom Thomas was one. The Ypres area had received 130mm (5 inches) of rain during August. Consequently, the battlefield was slick with mud and pockmarked with water-filled shell holes. It was easy for men to disappear. It would not be until March 1918 that Thomas was reported killed. The official date of death was given as 26 August – probably the last time anyone could recall seeing him alive. He is remembered at Tyne Cot Memorial.

When George Todd was reported as killed in the *Southern Reporter* in November 1917, people spoke well of him describing him as a quiet man.[47] His life had been unremarkable until the declaration of war. He was born in the Berwickshire village of Edrom in 1879. In 1906, he married Janet Scott, a farm outworker. George's employment was variously described as farm servant, estate worker and forester. By 1915, he and Janet had moved to West Morriston, 2 miles from Earlston. That year he enlisted in the 2nd Battalion King's Own Scottish Borderers and was killed in action on 4 October 1917. It would be over a year later that Janet received official notification of her husband's death. The *Berwickshire News and General Advertiser* paid tribute to her, noting: 'She has borne up very bravely during a year of trying suspense.'[48]

Janet never remarried and lived out her final days in a care home in Galashiels. She died in 1959 aged 84. George is remembered at Tyne Cot Memorial.

Two weeks after George died, Thomas Vallance, another Earlstonian, died of wounds received during the Battle of Passchendaele.

Thomas was born in Smailholm, a village a few miles from Earlston. By the age of 14, he was already working as a farm servant. In 1912, aged 27, he married Euphemia Simpson, a domestic servant who lived in Redpath. They set up home together in Redpath and Thomas got a job as a quarryman at the nearby quarry. Their first child, John, was born in March 1913, and their second, Elizabeth, was born in 1915.

Thomas first enlisted in the Argyll and Sutherland Highlanders before being transferred to the Seaforth Highlanders. In 1917, during the Battle of Passchendaele, he was wounded and died on 17 October.

He is buried at Bucquoy Road Cemetery, Ficheux, and also remembered on the family grave in Earlston Parish Church, along with Euphemia, who died in 1974, and their daughter Elizabeth, who died in 1999. It is thought that Thomas' son John died in 1982.

Passchendaele continued to take its toll on Earlston menfolk. Nine days after Thomas' death, Walter Slassor and James Weatherston were killed in action on the opening day of the Second Battle of Passchendaele.

Usually, when a man enlisted, the event was reported in a local newspaper. Similarly, when he was reported missing, died of wounds or killed, the news would be published. For Walter Slassor, that was not the case.

Walter was born in 1886, in Northumberland, the son of a shepherd. Fifteen years later he was working as a stone mason's labourer in Whittingham, Northumberland. By the age of 25, he was working as a gardener, then three years later he married Ann Scott in Tynemouth. The following year, 1915, Walter was living and working on the Earl of Haddington's Mellerstain Estate, just outside Earlston.

He enlisted in the Northumberland Fusiliers and, by 1917, found himself in Passchendaele. Initially, he was reported as missing, as an army report dated 8 December shows.[49] The report also shows that Ann was still living on the Mellerstain Estate. However, in a follow-up report dated 20 December[50], Walter is reported killed, and Ann had moved to Walker-on-Tyne. His official date of death was 26 October 1917.

The only newspaper report about Walter was the Weekly Casualty List, published on 11 December 1917, by the War Office.[51] Even then his first name was wrongly reported as 'William'.[52] The names of the fallen were read out in Earlston Parish Church in January 1919. Walter is remembered at Tyne Cot Memorial.

James Weatherston was 19 when he was killed during the Battle of Passchendaele. on 26 October 1917. He was the only son of James and Margaret Weatherston, who ran a grocery shop on the High Street, in Earlston. James had enlisted in the Army Service Corps Motor Transport Section in 1916, but was later transferred to the London Regiment (Royal Fusiliers).

James's death is something of a mystery. We know that he was a member of the 2nd Battalion Royal Fusiliers and that his battalion was involved in the battles of Passchendaele. We know from the 2nd Battalion War Diaries that, on 26 October 1917, the battalion was at Blairville No. 2 Camp. There is a single line entry that reads, 'Brigade practice ceremonial at 10 a.m. Sports in afternoon'.[53]

We know that whatever caused James's death, his body was not recovered. Consequently, he is remembered on the Tyne Cot Memorial, rather than at Tyne Cot Cemetery.

An announcement appeared in the *Scotsman* on 17 November, stating that James had been killed in action.

Before the outbreak of war, John Dickson had been living with his parents, Alexander and Helen, and his younger brother George, at his parent's house on Thorn Street, Earlston. John worked at the tweed mill, and it was there that he met Agnes Douglas. The two married in 191,3 and their first son, Alexander, was born the following year. A second son, James, was born in 1917. The baby's registration of birth shows that John was a corporal in the 1/4th King's Own Scottish Borders and, significantly, he did not register the birth, which was done by Agnes, so John might have been serving abroad when James was born.

On 8 November, John was standing in the dunes on Ras Abu Ameire Ridge, looking over the Mediterranean. His battalion, with the rest of the 155th Brigade, was to attack the Turks in what became known as the Battle of Wadi el Hesi.

The battle commenced at 2.20 p.m. under heavy enemy bombardment. The British artillery monitors couldn't locate the enemy guns, and so the shelling continued unchallenged. Just 1 hour and 40 minutes after the attack started, it was stopped as they waited for reinforcements. In those 100 minutes, the British sustained 285 casualties, including John. He is buried in Gaza War Cemetery. John's widow, Agnes, left Earlston with her two boys to live in Selkirk. It's not known if John ever saw his second son James.

The scale in the number of casualties sustained by the Allies was unprecedented. Consequently, a medical evacuation chain to deal with the wounded was developed. At the front, stretcher-bearers recovered the wounded, or helped the walking wounded to the nearest field ambulance.

A field ambulance was not a vehicle, but a mobile medical unit, and provided bearer posts and main and advanced dressing stations.

The field ambulance ensured that a wounded soldier was in a condition to be evacuated to a Casualty Clearing Station (CCS), the first, large, well-equipped, static medical facility that a casualty would encounter. Each CCS could accommodate up to 1,000 victims. All were equipped to perform major operations, including amputations.

Each had facilities and staff to diagnose and treat a range of medical conditions. A CCS would be established near a railhead so that cases requiring additional or long-term treatment could be evacuated to a base hospital.

In France and Flanders Britain had established 57 Casualty Clearing Stations. Each CCS was static, although not permanent. It would move to wherever that needs of the war dictated.

For example, between April 1916 and March 1917, Casualty Clearing Station No. 21 was located at Corbie. It was then relocated to Nesle until June 1917. It moved another five times before the end of the war, when it was moved to Bonn in Germany.[54] Casualty Clearing Station No. 21 is noteworthy because Wilfred Owen, the war poet, was treated there when it was located at Nesle.

Another casualty to receive treatment at 21 CCS was Robert Lees. Robert was born in 1881, in Makerstoun, Roxburghshire, to John and Maggie Lees. He attended the village school in Blainslie, Lauder, before becoming a ploughman like his father. However, by 1910, Robert had moved to Dalmeny, Linlithgowshire, where he was employed as a forester. It was there that he met Margaret Wilson Anthony, a domestic servant. They were married on 28 November 1913, at Crammond Bridge, Dalmeny.

On 15 September 1916, when working as a forester on the Arniston Estate near Gorebridge, Robert enlisted in King's Own Scottish Borders, serving in the 1st Battalion.

He served with the British Expeditionary Force in France and Flanders from 21 June 1917, and on 20 November 1917, saw the start of the Battle of Cambrai, which involved his battalion. On 25 November Robert was severely wounded by shrapnel from an exploding shell. He was evacuated to Casualty Clearing Station No. 21 at Ytres, but died of his wounds later that day.

He is buried at the Rocquigny-Equancourt Road British Cemetery, Manancourt.

A Village at War

Throughout the year, newspapers published a weekly report of the names of the wounded, as well as the dead. These lists offered readers an idea of the scale of the slaughter. For example, the *Southern Reporter* announced the following casualties from Earlston, just one small village:

> Private Robert Armstrong, KOSB, Redpath, missing, was formerly employed by Mr Adam Shortreed, Redpath, West End.
>
> Private Robson White, KOSB, West End, Earlston, missing, was a ploughman and has a wife with one child.
>
> Private George Young, KOSB, (married), reported missing, is a son of Mr Archibald Young, bootmaker.
>
> Private Alex Wilson, KOSB, second son of Mr Thomas Wilson, Janefield, has been severely wounded in the shoulder and head.
>
> Private John Young, KOSB, eldest son of Mr William Young, Station Road, has been severely wounded in head.
>
> Private Stewart Darling, KOSB, wounded, son of Mrs Darling, Greenlaw, late of Redpath.
>
> Private William Bell, KOSB, wounded, is the son of Mr Thomas Bell, Town Farm.
>
> Trooper James Taylor, Australians, wounded, is the eldest son of Mr Andrew Taylor, grocer, East Green.
>
> Private W Frater, Royal Scots has been severely wounded in leg below knee.

> Lance corporal James Rodgers, Argyll and Sutherland, husband of Mrs Rodgers, Earlston, has been killed in action, aged 28, he enlisted early last year.[55]

For villagers, especially those with loved ones in the military, this weekly list of the dead and wounded must have been upsetting to read.

Despite these lists, people must have been given hope that their loved one would return, just like the men in khaki who could be seen in the village enjoying their leave from the front.

In September, Robert Burns, the army reservist and member of the 16th Lancers, had returned on leave. He had been one of the first to mobilize, but here he was, a sergeant, who had survived the campaigns in France unscathed, although he did admit that he may have had, 'Hairbreadth escapes in the deadly trenches for even cavalrymen have to take their turn in trenchwork'.

The Men's Committee, 'considered that the war might last over another Christmas', and so organized a fundraising concert in the Corn Exchange Hall in late October.

The concert aimed to raise money to buy Christmas presents for Earlston men serving in the military. Christmas parcels had been sent to the men the previous year. However, those bound for soldiers in Egypt and Mesopotamia had taken too long to arrive. This year it was decided to send each man serving in these regions a postal order for 12 shillings and 6 pence. This solution had the benefit that, if the ship carrying this mail were sunk, the Government would refund the committee, which could then send another mail.

For those serving in Europe, or who were home on leave or wounded, each man received a shirt, a pair of socks, a towel, a Selkirk bannock, a cake of soap, a writing pad, a tin of health salts, a book, a

Christmas card, cigarettes and chocolate. Men who had never served abroad got a similar parcel, with some 'small exceptions'.[56]

The committee announced the introduction of a scheme to enable the people of Earlston and its parish to send their parcels at uniform and reduced rates on the first Wednesday of each month, to men serving abroad who were on the committee's Christmas parcel list.

Chapter 6

1918

New Year was heralded in a sombre mood compared to the pre-war years. The high cost of alcohol, plus Government restrictions on pub-opening hours, did not help, nor did the mill closing for a week's unpaid holiday. An impromptu dance was held at the Corn Exchange Hall to raise funds for the War Guild. However, after 'the bells had been rung' most folks didn't bother with first footin', but simply made their way home.

The last auction of 1917 at the Earlston Auction Mart was reported in the early editions of the local press in January and was read with interest.[57] That sale had been the first to be held under the Maximum Prices Order, which was legislation introduced by the Government under the Defence of the Realm Act, to control inflation and reduce poverty by making goods affordable.[58]

For cattle, sheep or pigs, the livestock was graded and the maximum price set for each grade by the Government. The Order was hard on butchers who now had to pay a charge to the auctioneer.

The Maximum Prices Order was used for raw materials too. In June of 1917, for example, the War Department advised farmers of an Order that had been made in April of that year, prohibiting the sale of wool grown in Great Britain, Ireland and the Isle of Man. The Order cancelled any contracts that might have been in place between farmers and buyers. Wool could only be sold to the Government's Director of Army Contracts.

The Order set a maximum price that was 50 per cent higher than the 1914 market rate, regardless of whether that value was realistic. Farmers were faced with a dilemma: should they sow grass to raise sheep? Grass seed was now twice as expensive as it had been in pre-war years, and in any event, land could be requisitioned for ploughing. But if the farmers did raise sheep, the fleeces could be requisitioned by the Government and existing contracts with dealers cancelled.

Other food staples also cost more. Eggs were scarce and, as a result, costly. Butter was also expensive, and salted butter was no longer available. Whereas people may have kept a few hens to supplement their diet or earn a little extra money, the cost of feeding the birds was now so expensive that the hens were disposed of.

Fodder for cattle was also expensive, leading to a scarcity of animals bred for beef. 'Meatless' days were becoming the norm for many families, and local papers published handy tips on how to cook items that had not previously appeared on menus. Unlike city dwellers, villagers had an abundant supply of potatoes and oatmeal, whereas bakers could supply barley-meal bannocks.

The School Board, in conjunction with the County Food Economy Committee, organized cookery demonstrations by a cook from the Ministry of Food. The sessions aimed to offer advice on, 'Dealing with the purchase, preparation and cookery of rationed foods and their substitutes'. The demonstrations were held in the village public school and seem to have been well attended and received.

On 5 February 1918, the Berwickshire Food Committee made an announcement that was carried by the local press, advising residents that food rationing would be adopted in Berwickshire, commencing 18 March. The bulletin warned, for the time being, rationed food items would be butter, margarine and tea, but rationing would be extended in due course. The advice included how householders, domestic servants and lodgers should apply. Additionally, there was guidance for retailer registration.

The announcement was not unexpected. The Government had established the Food Ministry in 1916, to promote voluntary rationing, but that had failed and so the compulsory scheme was introduced, first in London and the Home Counties then, from February, nationwide.

Eventually, meat, fats and sugar would be rationed, and householders would be allocated to particular butchers and grocers.

Bread was not rationed, although specific regulations, made under the Defence of the Realm Act, applied. For example, all bread had to be made from wholegrain flour; feeding bread to wild animals and birds was not permitted; and bread had to be at least 12 hours old before it could be sold to the public. This last requirement was introduced since bread is easier to slice thinly when cold.

Concerns were raised about the impact on the sick person's diet. For example, an anonymous letter published in the *Scotsman* noted that sufferers from tuberculosis needed 'a generous allowance of fattening foods'.

Breaches of the Rationing Order were dealt with in the courts, and the convictions were published in the press. The consequences were quite severe. A case heard in Hendon, concerning 'Unlawfully obtaining and using rationing books', resulted in 3 months' imprisonment. Another example, where an individual was charged with 'Being a retailer selling to unregistered customer', resulted in a £72 fine, with £5 5s costs.

And it wasn't just food that was rationed – coal was also subject to quotas, and one consequence of the high price of coal was the effect on town gas.

In June a national newspaper reported that the Earlston Gas Company was raising the price of gas by 10d per 1,000ft^3 of gas.[59]

Since the outbreak of the war, the cost of gas had increased by 40 per cent. Little wonder that the company had seen a decline in the consumption of gas by its customers.

In another report in the *Berwickshire News and General Advertiser*, a spokesperson for the company told the newspaper that: 'The increase was due to the high price of coal and labour, and moreover dividends must be seen to, that they lose not their substantial character and cease to attract'.[60]

From a company perspective the increase was too little, too late and the following month the directors were forced to announce that, since the profits for the year stood at a little over 12 shillings, no dividend would be paid.

U-boats continued to wreak havoc with shipping. For most people, a shortage of food was the most obvious impact, but for the families of the merchant seaman that crewed the cargo ships, the effect was personal.

James Brockie was born in Legerwood, a village a few miles from Earlston, in July 1891. James's father, Alexander Brockie was a coachman, and he and his wife, Margaret, moved to Union Street in Glasgow, where James joined the merchant navy as an engineer.

On 3 March, the SS *Northfield*, with James serving as Second Engineer, was torpedoed by U-boat *U60* off Lundy Island, when on passage from Glasgow to Devonport with a cargo of coal. The ship sank with the loss of all hands.

James is commemorated on the family gravestone in Earlston churchyard (see Figure 14), and remembered on the Merchant Navy Tower Hill Memorial in London.

Figure 14. Family headstone in Earlston churchyard commemorating James Brockie.

On the same day that James Brockie drowned, the Brest-Litovsky Treaty was signed, officially bringing to an end the war between Russia and Germany.

Germany had for some time been acutely aware of the impact that the USA sending troops to Europe would have on the outcome of the war, and more and more Americans arrived in Europe in 1918. Germany needed to complete its objective of capturing Paris soon, and so this Treaty allowed Germany to redeploy men from the Russian front to Flanders. The war with Russia had been mobile, with no great reliance on the trench system used in France and Flanders.

Instead, the Germans had perfected the use of 'shock' troops, and this tactic would be used to great advantage. But fortunately for the Allies, it would not be sustainable. Nonetheless, Earlston would lose a number of its menfolk in 1918.

On 7 February, a meeting of the West District Berwickshire County Council was convened in Earlston courtroom. The main item on the agenda for discussion was a scheme to settle disabled soldiers in rural communities, which was being implemented by the Board of Agriculture.[61]

An earlier scheme had proposed building villages in the district, but separate from existing communities, to house disabled soldiers and their families. This plan was rejected on economic grounds. Instead, this new scheme aimed to provide a way for disabled soldiers to earn a living. It was not, the spokesman of the board explained, meant for men who had come out of the war able-bodied, but rather for men whose health has been impaired by the war, and who were unable to carry out occupations in the towns. This description suggests that the scheme included the physically disabled, as well as men who were suffering from mental-health problems, such as post-traumatic stress disorder, or 'shell shock', as it was known then.

It was proposed that about 50 disabled men would be integrated into the village and that half of the men would be married. Disused houses would be repaired or renovated to accommodate the married men and their families, although it was conceded that some new builds might be required. The single men would be lodged with families in the village, thereby providing the hosts with extra cash. The men would be provided with land, 'for intensive cultivation such as market gardening or fruit cultivation. Able-bodied men would receive about 15 acres whereas disabled men anything between a good-sized garden to three or four acres'.

Dr Shirra Gibb, the County Council medical officer, suggested that the men and women from the village, who were then serving in the army, navy or air force, or working in the munitions factories, should be encouraged to return to the village as and when they were discharged. Alexander Lyal, a local farmer and member of the Council, suggested that the men be absorbed into farms to ease the chronic shortage of manpower. The spokesperson said that the purpose of the scheme was to offer disabled men a means to earn a living, not to resolve the workforce shortages.

It was agreed to set up a small committee to investigate the scheme, but it was doomed to failure. Only two weeks later, another group, the Allotments Society, held a meeting to identify suitable ground for allotments, where householders could grow fruit and vegetables. This group was more successful since, in April, it had secured an acre of land on Haughhead Farm. There were 18 applications for 16 allotments.

The following week the farmer who owned the fields that formed the Earlston Golf Course advised the club that he had received instructions to plough the course for crops. The club announced its intention to let the club lapse until after the war. Meantime, the farmer could not muster the manpower for ploughing.

The situation was not helped by an announcement from the Board of Agriculture regarding the recruitment of farm labourers. But that was still two months away.

On 14 November 1914, the Heart of Midlothian Football Club (Hearts) had entertained Falkirk. Hearts were league leaders and looked to be on their way to another victory. The news from Flanders and France was not so positive, with the British Expeditionary Force looking at defeat, and the Queen's Own Cameron Highlanders regiment used the halftime period to appeal for volunteers. The initial responses were not good. However, by full-time, several men had stepped forward, including the Hearts' winger James Speedie.

The *Evening Dispatch* carried an article about Speedie's decision under the headline: Three Hearts men with the Colours now. Two days later, the *Evening News* printed a letter from 'a Soldier's Daughter', in which she suggested that, 'While Hearts continue to play football, enabled thus to pursue their peaceful play by the sacrifice of the lives of thousands of their countrymen, they might adopt, temporarily, a nom de plume, say "The White Feathers of Midlothian".'[62]

A week later, MP Sir George McCrae held a press conference in the Hearts boardroom, at which he announced that eleven Hearts players had enlisted in his new battalion, the 16th Royal Scots. The next day McCrae told reporters that recruitment would start on Friday, 27 November, but the campaign lasted only seven days.

McCrae was a born leader who, far from insisting that young men should go to fight, invited them to join him. He went on to say, 'I would not, I could not, ask you to serve unless I share the danger at your side'.

Within a week McCrae had his battalion of over 1,300 men. And it wasn't just Hearts' players and their supporters who joined, but also players and supporters from teams such as Hibernian, Dunfermline, Falkirk and Raith Rovers. In all, over 75 clubs provided volunteers. Then other sportsmen started to join: rugby players, golfers and athletes enlisted in what became known as 'McCrae's Battalion'.

The McCraes first saw action in January 1916, however, by May 1918 and after suffering heavy losses, the battalion was reduced to cadre strength, and in August that year, it was disbanded.

James William Robertson enlisted in the 16th Battalion. He was living in Edinburgh and may have been a Hearts supporter, but in any event, he was employed as a gardener. James was born in Balmerino, Fife, but his parents moved to Earlston in the late 1880s, when James senior obtained a job as a gardener at Cowdenknowes House, where James William became a gardener too. In 1912, James married Catherine Tully, a factory worker, who was born and raised in Earlston. The couple lived on Station Road, in Earlston.

James was killed on 21 March 1918, during the Battle of St Quentin. His body was not recovered from the battlefield, and he is remembered at the Arras Memorial.

On the last Saturday of February 1915, when the shop was shuttered and locked, a small presentation was held in the Earlston Cooperative Store. Two bakers, John Wilkie and David Lunam, had enlisted in the Army Service Corps and this was their last working day.

Their colleagues had contributed to the purchase of pipes and tobacco as gifts for the two men. Mr Scott, the shop manager, presented the presents and made a small speech, thanking them both for their service and wishing them well on their new adventure.

John would survive the war, but David would not, but that was a couple of years away. He spent the remaining days at his home in Rodger's Place, Earlston, with his family – father David, mother Isabella, his two sisters Euphemia and Mary, and brother Thomas. He left for basic training on the following Wednesday and by July that year, David was in France, at a camp called Étaples.

David continued to serve as a baker for another two years until, in 1917, he was 'combed out' and transferred to the 13th Battalion of Yorkshire Regiment. In March the following year, the battalion suffered heavy casualties during the Battle of Étaples. David sustained a gunshot wound to his abdomen and was taken to No. 24 General Hospital, where he died on 27 March 1918. He is buried in Étaples Military Cemetery.

Was David's transfer to the Yorkshire Light Infantry just one of those random decisions made by military commanders, or was there something more sinister about the move? After all, why transfer a soldier into a regiment that he had no association with?

The Étaples Base was of great importance to the British Expeditionary Force, and served as an Infantry Base Depot, where supplies, brought in from the coast some 15 miles away, could be sorted, stored and dispatched to the front, wherever and whenever they were needed. The base also served as a staging post for men going to the front, transferring to other theatres of war, or for hospital treatment and convalescence. Between June 1915 and September 1917, more than a million officers and men passed through the base.

Conditions at the base were described as 'oppressive'. Men had to sleep in tents even though the base was permanent and food rations were at a minimum level. Passes to visit the nearby town of Étaples were heavily restricted.

Bullying and other forms of abuse were commonplace. The most notorious was the training ground, called the 'Bull Ring'. Such were the conditions here that wounded soldiers volunteered to return to the trenches before being cleared medically fit rather than face the Bull Ring.

In 1917, troops from Great Britain, Canada, Australia and New Zealand mutinied. Two men were killed by the military police: one beaten to death and the other shot.

The riots spread to Étaples, and it took considerable effort to restore control of the situation. Regiments took different measures to restore 'normality'. The 13th Battalion Yorkshire Regiment sentenced two sergeants to death for an attempt to organize a strike.

Perhaps placing men such as David, who was from outside the regiment's traditional recruiting areas, inside the battalions was an attempt to break the battalions' camaraderie. With the recent mutiny, such incomers would have been viewed as infiltrators and possible collaborators, their mere presence sowing seeds of doubt and suspicion. Their lives must have been hellish.

Food rationing was a visible sign that there needed to be an increase in food production and that labour was needed on farms, and yet farmworkers continued to be targeted by the recruiters.

On 20 April, the Board of Agriculture issued a 'Proclamation' withdrawing exemption from military service for farmers and farmworkers.[63]

Previously men of a certain age and medical category could be exempted by military tribunals because their continued work on farms was essential. This was overturned resulting in men of medical category 'A', and aged between 19 and 23, being eligible for call-up. Military tribunals could exempt these men only with the approval of the Board of Agriculture.

Farmers faced the possibility of losing their fittest, most able farmhands. It appears that the conflicting goals of needing more men for combat roles, thereby denying farms of much-needed labour, were becoming almost unmanageable. The medical categories referred to in the Proclamation were:

A. Able to march, see to shoot, hear well and stand active service conditions.
B. Free from serious organic diseases, able to stand service on Lines of Communication in France or in garrisons in the tropics.
C. Free from serious organic diseases, able to stand service in garrisons at home.
D. Unfit but could be fit within six months.

Each category was divided into subcategories, but these appear to have been very broad in scope. For example, Categories B and C had three subcategories, the most onerous of which was subcategory 1 which was defined as the ability to march 5 miles, see to shoot with glasses and hear well; subcategory 2 was defined as the ability to walk 5 miles, see and hear sufficiently for ordinary purposes; subcategory 3 was described as only suitable for sedentary work.

Farmers had relied on schoolboys to help with 'tattie howking', and this year their assistance was needed more than ever. A local newspaper reported a plea from the farming community that:

> The help of schoolboys in cereal and potato harvest is of such importance that it is hoped that the Scottish Education Department will not place any obstacle in the way of their employment at these seasons, their being set free from school for a short period of their needed assistance entailing little or no detriment to their education.

The Earlston Allotments Society had decided to rent a field at the east end of the village and notices were posted in shop windows advertising 300yd^2 allotments for a rent of 6 shillings.

Recruitment of men continued. In April, Thomas Wallace, an Earlston draper and clothier, appealed against the withdrawal of his exemption certificate. Thomas had been placed in Medical Category C3 – only suitable for sedentary work at a home garrison. The National Service Representative, as the military advisors were now known, agreed not to press the case against Thomas.

Another case heard at the same tribunal was that of John Archibald. John's brother, James, had been Earlston's first fatality on active service, their brother, Thomas, had been wounded, and John had been granted a certificate of exemption until a replacement could be found. John's case had been subject to review sixteen times, including the occasion when John's father had explained that a replacement had been found, but inexplicably the authorities had sent the man to Ireland. Sheriff Chisholm, who was presiding over this case, dismissed John's appeal.

The next case was that of Thomas Taylor, a grocer and van man for his father's grocery business. Since Thomas was now 19 years old and classified as medically 'A1', Thomas's exemption was withdrawn. Having just heard how long it was taking to find a replacement for John Archibald, Taylor's father asked: 'What am I do to?'

Sheriff Chisholm replied: 'That, I am afraid, I don't know. You will have to see if you can get someone else in his place.'

One agricultural worker who did enlist was Adam Wilson. Adam was a ploughman, born in Gordon, a village a few miles from Earlston. He enlisted in the Army Service Corps in 1915, serving as a driver until he was transferred to the London Regiment (Artists Rifles), at the rank of Rifleman. In April 1918, he was reported missing, but in May, the *Hawick News and Border Chronicle* announced that he was now reported to have died from his wounds as a prisoner of war in Germany.[64] He is buried at the Niederzwehren Cemetery, in Kassel.

Why Adam should be remembered on the Earlston war memorial is a mystery, since neither he nor his parents had any direct connection with the village. The nature of agricultural work meant a somewhat nomadic life for Adam's family, as can be judged from the places of birth recorded for Adam and his six siblings. Margaret Wilson, Adam's mother, had seven children in the first sixteen years of marriage to Alexander Wilson. The children were born at Melrose, Gordon, Greenlaw, Eccles and Selkirk, with and the two youngest born at Cavers. It doesn't appear that Adam worked on any of Earlston's farms.

The Simpson family were patriots. Helen, the matriarch, had seven children and five of them enlisted. Her eldest son Alexander, or 'Sandy', enlisted as soon as war was declared. Three other sons – John, Andrew and George –would follow. Her eldest daughter Jessie joined the Women's Auxiliary Army Corps when it was formed in 1917. Daughter Elizabeth and son Robert remained at home, working on the farm at Fans.

Sandy joined the 11th (Service) Battalion Argyll and Sutherland Highlanders and was shipped to France the following year. He fought hard: he was wounded twice, sustaining a gunshot wound to the head (1915) and to his thigh (1917); and played hard (he lost his Lance Corporal stripe for drunkenness, although he later won it back).

He was awarded the Military Medal for Conspicuous Bravery in the Field in 1918. But later that year, on 20 April, Sandy was killed in action in Arras.

Helen Simpson had nursed her husband Andrew for two months as he fought cancer, until he finally succumbed to the ravages of the disease in late 1916. Now her eldest son had died fighting, not cancer, but for King and Country.

Helen was naturally keen to have Sandy's bravery medal as a tangible reminder of the son she had lost. She asked her minister, Reverend Cameron, to contact the War Office on her behalf, requesting that Sandy's medal be sent to her. The reply from the War Office (Infantry Records) was as surprising as it was cold: 'I regret that I have no record of a Military Medal awarded to the late S/3647 Pte. Simpson.'

The Reverend Cameron's reply was terse: 'The award of the Military Medal was gazetted by the War Office officially on the 12/6/18, so you must have missed it.'

The official response was without apology for the denial of the record of Sandy's medal, for failing to give him his correct rank, or for the distress caused. Instead, it merely stated: 'I have to inform you that this had now been verified, and will be disposed of when the necessary authority is received from the War Office.'

The words 'disposed of' must have been offensive to Helen.

As part of its public relations campaign, the War Office invited Helen to receive Sandy's medal at a public presentation. She declined for health reasons.

In December 1918, months after the exchange of letters began, Helen finally received the treasured medal. However, the War Office continued its unsympathetic manner to the end. With the medal, Helen received a form to sign to acknowledge receipt and that, 'I further declare that, in the event of the medal being lost, stolen or destroyed, no claim for replacement will be made against the public'.

Helen would not make a claim for the loss of the medal, nor for the loss of her irreplaceable son.

Despite the chain of correspondence, in 1921, the War Office was still attempting to send Sandy's campaign medals to a wrong address.[65]

Having been refused an exemption from the MILITARY TRIBUNAL in 1916, David Borthwick enlisted in McCrae's Battalion. The 16th Battalion was part of the 101st Brigade which, in turn, was part of the 34th Division. The battalion saw action at Arras and Ypres, and David was severely wounded at Passchendaele, in October 1916.

During the Battle of Lys, the 16th Battalion protected the land to the north-west of the town of Armentières. David had been shot in both legs and an arm when German soldiers captured him on 8 April. He was transferred to the German military hospital in Lille, but died of his wounds on 27 April 1918. He is buried in Lille Southern Cemetery.

John Young was born in Monkwearmouth, in County Durham, on 2 February 1898. His father, William, was a journeyman tailor, travelling the country to either find permanent employment or until he qualified as a master tailor, which would have allowed him to set up his own business.

William and his wife Margaret were both from the Earlston area (Channelkirk and Melrose, respectively), so it is no surprise that they settled in the village with John and his sister, Jane, who was his elder by three years.

The family lodged in a house on Station Road, with three other families. The Youngs had three more children at this address: sons William and George, and a daughter Mary. The house, which had only nine rooms with windows, had, according to the 1911 census, twenty-two people living there. When he left school, John took a job at the Simpson and Fairbairn tweed mill.

He enlisted in the 4th Battalion King's Own Scottish Borderers in early January 1914, with service number 4455. In May 1915, he was transferred to the Scottish Provisional Battalion. Provisional battalions were formed to supplement regular battalions that had been severely depleted due to high casualty rates. He was retransferred to the KOSB (service number 200280) at the end of March 1916.

1916 saw the introduction of conscription and active service for territorial battalions. As a consequence, the 4th and 5th Battalion KOSB and 4th and 5th Royal Scots Fusiliers formed the 155th Brigade, 52nd Lowland Division, which was deployed to the Middle East as part of the Egyptian Expeditionary Force.

On 17 April 1917, the Second Battle of Gaza commenced. The fighting was brutal and bloody, and at the end of the third day of action, the brigade, including John's battalion, had suffered almost 50 per cent casualties, including John, who was wounded in his upper right arm and on the right side of his head.

Three days later, John was evacuated to the military hospital in Alexandria, Egypt. There, doctors discovered that John's right humerus, the long bone in the upper arm, was shattered. An X-ray could find no trace of the bullet that had caused the head wound. The arm wound caused the most concern, due to the extent of the bone damage and that fact that the wound was suppurating.

On 26 April, John's condition was listed as 'dangerously ill'. He remained in this condition for over a month. During this time, John underwent two operations to explore and drain his wounds. He was also assessed by the medical staff, who initially concluded John was 'permanently unfit'. However, this initial assessment was scratched out in his medical report. Instead, the recommendation was that he return to Great Britain. Consequently, on 16 August 1917, John was evacuated to Great Britain on board the hospital ship HMHS *Formosa*. When the ship docked in Liverpool, on 5 September, John was admitted to a Liverpool hospital.

By the end of February 1918, John had been transferred to the 2nd Scottish General Hospital in Edinburgh. His Medical Report of 22 February noted that John was 'in good general health'. However, it also stated that his right arm and hand had limited movement. Also, the wounds on his arm had not healed, despite having undergone five operations to drain the wound and remove bone fragments. The report also notes that, 'He had a wound on the right side of the face, which causes him no trouble now'.

John was discharged from the army as being permanently unfit for military service of any sort, and discharged from hospital on 24 March. He returned to Earlston to be cared for by his family. Despite the Medical Board's conclusion that John's head wound was no cause for concern, John had developed an abscess on his brain at the site of the gunshot wound. As the effects of the abscess grew, caring for John must have been a particularly difficult time for the family. The abscess would most likely have caused dramatic changes to John's physical control and to his personality. Additionally, the infection was damaging his heart.

A few days before his death, he was transferred to Edinburgh Royal Infirmary. He died on Thursday, 20 June 1918. The cause of the death given on the registration of death was a temporo-sphenoidal abscess and ulcerative endocarditis – that is, a brain abscess and damaged heart.

John's burial took place on Sunday, 23 June 1918, in Earlston parish churchyard. The Earlston Company of Volunteers, under the command of Lieutenant Harvie, attended his funeral, and pipers and drummers from a detachment of Argyll and Sutherland Highlanders played laments (Figure 15).

Figure 15. Gravestone of John Fraser Young in Earlston churchyard.

In April, the Government launched the 'War Implements Investment Week' fundraising campaign. Towns and villages were encouraged to donate to the fund, which would allow the Government to purchase arms and munitions. Earlston set itself a target of £5,000, to finance the purchase of a tank. That week, villagers raised over £14,000, and, since the money was still being counted when the announcement was made, the village raised enough to purchase three tanks.

At the outbreak of the war, the full potential of the machine gun was not appreciated. Nonetheless, each battalion had a machine-gun section comprising two machine guns and sixteen men under the command of a lieutenant or second lieutenant.

The devastating capabilities were soon recognized, and machine-gun positions were prime targets for both sides. As a consequence, the Machine Gun Corps suffered a 50 per cent casualty rate earning the Corps the nickname 'The Suicide Club'.[66]

Thomas Gillie was the son of Thomas and Jessie (née Cockburn) Gillie, and was born in Coldingham, in 1895. Thomas, like his father, was a ploughman working at Middlethird Farm in Gordon.

In August 1915, Thomas enlisted in the 4th Battalion of the King's Own Scottish Borderers. Sometime later he was transferred to the Machine Gun Corps, Infantry Battalion.

During his military service Thomas, who was promoted to Lance Corporal, was wounded twice and had a lengthy stay in hospital to treat 'diarrhoea' (74 days). By 1918, Thomas was serving in the 12th Battalion, Machine Gun Corps, which was part of the 12th Division.

On 1 July 1918, two years to the day since the British offensive had opened on the Somme, the 12th Division attacked Bouzincourt. After initial success, a counterattack drove the attacking units back, at a cost of 680 casualties. One of those casualties was Thomas. He was wounded for a third time on 2 July, and evacuated to the 3rd Canadian Stationary Hospital, where he died of his wounds later that same day. His death was announced in the local press on 1 August 1918.[67]

John Boyd, who had enlisted in the King's Own Scottish Borderers as a 16 year old, joined the 4th Battalion Seaforth Highlanders in Berwick, in 1916.

During that year, John saw action at the Battle of the Ancre. The following year he fought in the First and Second Battles of the Scarpe, the capture and defence of Roeux, the Battle of Pilkem Ridge and the Battle of Menin Road Ridge. By 1918, John's battalion had also fought at the Battle of St Quentin, the Battle of Bapaume, the

A Village at War

Battle of Estaires and the Battle of Hazebrouck. For someone so keen to enlist, John indeed did his bit for King and Country.

In July, during the Battle of the Tardenois, one of the battles of the Marne, John sustained gunshot wounds and died on 24 July. He is buried in St Imoges churchyard.

On 6 July, it was King George V and Queen Mary's silver wedding anniversary, and Earlstonians were determined to celebrate it in style.

A gala day was held on Saturday at Carolside Gardens, starting at 2.30 p.m., with the Galashiels Town Band marching from the village square to Carolside. Several activities had been organized, including sports, tug-of-war, football, pillow fights, Aunt Sallies and swings, as well as a programme of songs and dances. Refreshments were provided but, due to rationing, visitors were advised to bring their own sugar. The event ended at Carolside at 7 p.m. and was followed by a fancy-dress parade, which started at 8 p.m. from the Corn Exchange. There were over 100 entries, and the village brass band headed the procession under the leadership of Samuel Fisher. The Clown Band brought up the rear.

The event proved to be a resounding success. Although there were other entertainments, such as the circus that set up its big top on the West Green a couple of weeks later, they did not compare with the gala day, and it was repeated as a Red Cross fundraiser in August.

The August event, again held at Carolside, had a similar programme to the July gala day, with the notable addition of a performance by the pipe band of the Argyll and Sutherland Highlanders. In the evening, following the fancy-dress parade, a dance in costume was held in the Corn Exchange and a special collection was taken for the newly inaugurated Local Prisoners of War Fund.

The first dozen years of the 1900s must have been exciting for the young and privileged. At a time when the fastest mode of personal travel was a galloping horse, there were now motorcycles and motorcars to whisk them around. And after the Wright brothers' famous flight at Kitty Hawk, in 1903, for the very privileged, aeroplanes were also a possibility.

William Barrie Young's upbringing was privileged by Earlston standards. His father was the village doctor, who could afford three live-in servants – a cook, a domestic servant and a coachman. However, there is no record of him owning a motorcycle or a car, let alone an aircraft.

William did not follow his father to medical school. Instead, in 1913, he became a Motor, Steam and Mechanical Engineering Apprentice at Waverley Engineering Works, in Galashiels. Initially, William joined the Lothian and Border Horse, but at the first opportunity transferred to the Royal Flying Corps.

His engineering expertise seemed to have been a prerequisite in his being accepted as a student pilot. George Miles Rodger, another of Earlston's aviators, also had an engineering background.

The Royal Flying Corp did not have training facilities. Instead, William trained at the Ruffy Baumann Flying School in Hendon, just outside London.

On 6 September 1915, William 'took his ticket' – that is, he sat his Royal Aero Club exam (see Figure 16). The exam comprised two distance flights in a closed circuit of at least 5 kilometres (3 miles, 185 yards), as well as one altitude flight at a minimum height of 50 metres (164 ft), which could form part of the two distance flights. The rules required that:

> The course for the distance flights should be marked out by two posts no more than 500metres (547 yards) apart. After each turn round one of the posts, the pilot must change the direction of flight when going round the second post, so the circuit is an uninterrupted series of figures of eight.

A Village at War

The method of alighting (landing) for each of the flights should be with the motor stopped at, or before, touching the ground. The aeroplane must come to rest within a distance of 50 metres (164ft) from a point previously indicated by the candidate.

And so, after meeting the required standard, William gained his Royal Aero Club Certificate (No. 1701) and was now a fully qualified pilot.

Figure 16. William Barrie Young's Aero Club Certificate photograph. (Public domain)

The pace of change in aviation technology at the time was rapid and remarkable: from the first powered flight to a weapon of war in little over ten years. However, the full usefulness of aircraft would not be realized until a couple of years into the war.

After enlisting, William was based at Brooklands Aerodrome from 10 September 1915. He transferred to No. 24 Squadron, which had been formed just nine days earlier, which was the world's first single-seat fighter squadron.

In early 1916, William was transferred to No. 20 Squadron, then attended machine-gun school for a month before moving to No. 12 Squadron.

Aerial dominance was not the primary objective, nor was bombing, since bomb loads were minimal. Instead, strategists and planners realized that the best way to identify the weaknesses in their opponent's defence was by aerial photography. Thus, the primary role of the Royal Flying Corps (RFC) was gathering intelligence.

William quickly qualified on several types of machines, including the main workhorse of the RFC, the Bristol F28 – the Bristol Fighter.

In March 1916, he qualified as an instructor pilot before returning to front-line duties. Flying those early aircraft was physically demanding. The controls were all manual and required a degree of strength to operate them. The cockpits were open, exposing the pilot to the elements, and were not heated. In addition, when flying at high altitude, there was no provision to supply the crew with oxygen.

In addition to the physical strain, the mental stress must have been draining. The fragility of the aircraft, being required to fly in weather not envisaged by the machines' designers, and the threat of attack by enemy aircraft would have taken its toll. That William survived from 1915 to 1918 is remarkable, since this was a period when a pilot had a life expectancy of six weeks.

Then on 20 October 1916, while flying on patrol over the Somme, his aircraft was attacked and William was severely wounded. Somehow, he managed to evade further attacks and landed at a French airfield to discover that his gunner/observer, 26-year-old 2nd Lieutenant Reginald Davis from Essex, had been killed. William had sustained a severe gunshot wound to his chest and was transferred to a hospital in Glasgow. For his actions on 20 October, he was mentioned in dispatches.

It would be almost a year later until William was declared fit and he was able to return to flying duties. He was transferred to School of Specialist Flying as an instructor and was soon promoted to Deputy Wing Exam Officer.

On 8 August 1918, William took off on a training flight, but what happened next was not ever established, other than there was a catastrophic failure of the aircraft, which spun out of control and smashed into the ground, killing William instantly.

The following Tuesday William was buried in Earlston parish churchyard (Figure 17). A guard of honour from the Argyll and Sutherland Highlanders accompanied the funeral cortège, and the pipe band from the same regiment played 'The Land o' the Leal' and 'The Flowers of the Forest'. A bugler played the 'Last Post' after the service.

Figure 17. The gravestone of William Barrie Young in Earlston churchyard.

  James Hardie was the son of John and Charlotte Hardie who lived on the High Street, Earlston, together with sisters Jane, Isabella, Joan and Betsy, and brother John. James had a long military career and served with the King's Own Scottish Borderers for ten years, the 8th Royal Scots for three years and the 60th Rifles for two years.
  In 1905, he married Jane Mathison Cleghorn of Galashiels and three years later their daughter, Jemima, was born. James emigrated to Canada, sailing on the SS *Columbia* and arriving in New York in

1910, before continuing his journey to Canada. Janet and Jemima emigrated the following year.

With his previous military experience, James enlisted with the 100th Winnipeg Grenadiers in 1915. Surprisingly, he was discharged after only three weeks because he was, 'unlikely to become efficient'.

Meanwhile, his brother John enlisted in the 1/4th Battalion, King's Own Scottish Borderers and was deployed to Gallipoli in 1915. He was one of the many casualties of the Achi Babu Nullah attack on 12 July 1915.

John's death may have spurred James to re-enlist. He joined the Canadian Mounted Rifles, and despite the previous reservations of his ability to become efficient, he rose to the rank of Company Sergeant Major.

On 15 August 1916, James was shipped to Europe with the rest of the 128th Battalion, Canadian Expeditionary Force.

On 14 September 1918, James was reported missing in action. Five months later, a soldier who had been in James's platoon, contacted his wife and told her that he had seen James killed. He is remembered at Vimy Memorial.

Henry Duff was another Earlstonian who emigrated to Canada (see Figure 18). Son of Archibald Duff, a shoemaker, and his wife, Helen, Henry worked as a draper's assistant. Henry's sister, Annie, had moved to Canada and was living in Toronto when Henry sailed onboard the SS *Hesperian* from Glasgow, arriving in Quebec on 19 May 1914.

On 7 December the following year, Henry reported to the Toronto Recruiting Depot to enlist in the 92nd Overseas Battalion (Highlander), Canadian Expeditionary Force. He had previously served for a year with the Camp Guard at the Kapuskasing Internment Camp in Ontario. After six months' training, Henry sailed from Halifax on 20 May, on board the SS *Empress of Britain*, arriving in England on 29 May 1916.

Figure 18. Henry Duff (Source: Sheila MacKay)

Like many other men, Henry was affected by the poor conditions in the trenches. He was hospitalized on several occasions for eczema, scabies and an abscess on his gum. Henry was granted leave to return to Great Britain from 27 October until 8 November 1916, no doubt to spend time with his parents in Earlston.

When his father, Archibald, died on 25 January 1918, Henry did not return home for his funeral. However, when his mother died later that year, he attended her funeral before rejoining his unit.

Henry was killed in action on 27 September when, to save the lives of his comrades, he single-handedly attempted to destroy a machine-gun crew. A companion noted, 'It was the bravest deed I have ever seen in the war'. He is buried in the Sains-les-Marquion British Cemetery.

In March 1918, the war between Germany and Russia had ended with the signing of the Brest-Litovsk Treaty. Germany had then redeployed her troops from the Eastern Front to Flanders and France. As a consequence, Germany had been able to make a breakthrough on the Somme. But now the Allies were starting to push back, and with the threat of more American troops arriving in Europe, on 4 October, Germany asked the Allies to sign an Armistice Agreement.

Saturday, 12 October 1918, was just another day in the war for Willie Kerr. He and his battalion, the 6th Seaforth Highlanders, were stationed near the Belgium town of Naves. It was rumoured that the war could soon be over: the Germans had contacted President Wilson, but for the troops on the ground, it was a pipe dream.

Unlike Willie's civilian days working in the Commercial Bank on Earlston's High Street, every day in the army was a workday. This Saturday was no different. The commanding officer held a mid-morning conference with all company commanders, and at 11 a.m. Willie's battalion was instructed to move to the brigade reserve position.

Back home in Earlston, Willie's father was busy with his joinery business, while his mother, Annie, was most likely taking a well-earned break from housework and sitting down to a mid-morning cup of tea.

At midday, the 5th Battalion Seaforth Highlanders and 6th Gordon Highlanders started the attack. Willie and his mates would have been praying that the attack would be successful so they would not be called upon.

By mid-afternoon, Annie was thinking about preparing the evening meal, whereas William's father was thinking about finishing work and heading home for the day.

Willie's battalion was moved again, closer to the front line.

The enemy started to shell Willie's position using high explosive shells and 'blue-cross' gas.

By evening, his battalion had suffered three casualties: Second Lieutenant Rennie, Willie and another unknown private. Willie died of his wounds later that night.

In Earlston, William senior and his wife Annie retired to bed, perhaps looking forward to meeting family and friends when they attended church in the morning, but certainly blissfully unaware that their youngest son had been killed.

Willie was buried in Queant Communal Cemetery British Extension, and is remembered on the family gravestone in Earlston churchyard (Figure 19), and on the Earlston war memorial.

Four weeks later, on 11 November, the Armistice Agreement was signed and hostilities were suspended.

Three days later Willie's death was announced in a local newspaper.[68]

Figure 19. Family gravestone in Earlston churchyard commemorating Willie Kerr.

In pre-war years there was quite a social life, with the village boasting an orchestra, which was regularly employed at musical evenings and operatic shows. The school plays and operettas involved a substantial number of villagers, in addition to the school staff and pupils. A newspaper review of the production of *The Magic Ruby*, mentioned earlier, notes that Archibald Black junior was cast as 'Ah Sin', a Chinese servant.

Archibald Snr also seems to have been active in village social life; for example, he was secretary of the Ercildoune Burns' Club. However, his other children – Alexander, Jane, Alice, Herriot and Jessie – along with his wife Alice, do not seem to have been so active.

Young Archibald attended 'Continuation Classes', a forerunner of modern-day evening classes. In 1914, he received a prize for 1st-year physics. In 1915, he was awarded a prize for arithmetic.

Quite what career path a budding actor/singer/physicist would have followed isn't recorded. However, we know that Archibald joined the KOSB and, since the minimum age was 18 years, that would make his year of enlistment 1917.

Sometime over the next twelve months, Archibald was transferred to the Labour Corps. Formed in January 1917, the Corps had grown to some 390,000 men – or 10 per cent of the total size of the army – by Armistice Day. The Corps was manned by officers and men who were deemed to be below 'A1' medical condition, the level of fitness needed for front-line service. In April 1917, several infantry divisions were transferred to the Corps, so that might have been when Archibald was moved from the KOSBs.

The Labour Corps served a vital role, yet it was always regarded as an inferior organization by the army as a whole, and the men who died are commemorated under their original regiment, with the Labour Corps being secondary. For example, Archibald is remembered on his Commonwealth War Graves headstone in Awoingt British Cemetery and on the Earlston war memorial as a private in the KOSB.

Archibald contracted pneumonia and died in a French hospital 24 October 1918, just three weeks before the Armistice was declared.

Archibald may have contracted flu, which then developed into pneumonia. Since January 1918, flu had been spreading throughout Europe. Soldiers, because of the primitive conditions in the trenches, were susceptible to infectious diseases. Men would develop sore throats, headaches and a loss of appetite. Usually, recovery was quick, and the British doctors called it the 'three-day fever' (the French nicknamed it 'la grippe'). However, as the virus spread through the population, it mutated into a deadly form. Someone who was hale and hearty at breakfast could be dead by dinner time. There were no treatments for flu, and no antibiotics to treat pneumonia.

Censorship at the time prevented newspapers reporting the spread of the disease for fear of affecting the morale of the population. It wasn't until the King of Spain became a casualty that the news broke, and the outbreak became known as 'Spanish flu'.

Hundreds of thousands of men returning home after the Armistice had been signed helped to spread the virus, which would kill 50 million people worldwide. A quarter of the population of Great Britain would be affected, resulting in 228,000 deaths.

In Earlston, the infection started to take effect in early summer, resulting in the public school being closed for an extended period. Dr Young, the village doctor, reported sixty cases of flu among the pupils. Seven villagers died of influenza/pneumonia in 1918.

The county medical officer offered 'influenza hints' to readers of the local newspapers. Some of the advice is valid today such as: 'Avoid scattering infection in sneezing and coughing'; and 'Stay in bed until all fever is gone'. Other advice would probably not be followed today, such as, 'Gargle the throat with a solution of one in 5,000 permanganates of potassium in water containing a pinch of common salt'.

The article also recommends: 'If one gets home wet or chilled a glass hot lemonade or a warm bath should be taken immediately'. For many villagers, and indeed farmworkers, a warm bath meant stoking up a good fire, carrying pails of water from the nearest tap (usually outside) and heating the water over the fire. A tin bath was placed in the middle of the kitchen floor then filled with hot water. Not a situation recognizable today.

On 11 November 1918, Germany signed the Armistice, which brought the war to an end.

When the news reached Earlston, the mill 'buzzer' was sounded, advising villagers that something unusual had happened. This signal was followed by the ringing of the bells of the parish church and the Corn Exchange.

A large Union Jack was flown above the mill and flags appeared on the High Street. Workers at the mill were given a half-day holiday and, at midday, the Reverend Walter Davidson held a service of thanks at the parish church, which was well attended.

That evening an impromptu concert was held at the Corn Exchange under the auspices of the Discharged Sailors and Soldiers Federation.

In late December, three Earlston men, who had been taken prisoner, arrived back in Earlston. Adam Mather, the tailor's son and James Adler, whose parents lived in Coldstream, had worked for a period of their captivity behind German lines, where they had been exposed to Allied artillery fire. George Watson, a ploughman from Yarlside Farm, had been wounded, but had been treated well at a German hospital for three months. When he was deemed fit enough, he was put to work in a coal mine near the Friedrichsfeld Camp. All three men talked of starvation and hard work during their captivity.

Another repatriated prisoner of war (POW) was John Dunlop, a private in 16th Royal Scots. John's family had moved to Earlston from Gordon in 1917. John had been wounded in his right arm and left shoulder when he was captured in March 1917. He told how he was marched through France for three days before being forced into a railway wagon. He estimated that the train consisted of 300 wagons with about 60 prisoners forced into each one. The men were in the wagons for three days and only allowed to leave the wagon once during that time, for soup and water. He recalled that there was hardly standing room, so the discomfort can be imagined.

He was sent to Münster POW camp, and told how the food was 'utterly bad', but this was alleviated by being given access to football pitches and concert halls.

After four months he was sent to work in a coal mine near Hamm. John was fortunate in as much as his wounds prevented him from being assigned hard manual work. The men were subjected to brutal treatment, with frequent beatings by rifle butts. He described the food as 'wretched'. After his imprisonment, John was transferred to Minden Hospital before being sent to Switzerland as a wounded prisoner.

Before leaving Minden, he began to receive food parcels and recalled receiving six packages in the space of two days. However, at the frontier, everything was taken from the men, with spurious reasons given for the confiscation. For example, new boots were confiscated because they might contain secret documents in their soles. The socks that John was wearing when he entered Switzerland were the same pair he had been wearing when he had been taken prisoner six months earlier and they had only been once washed during that time. He was happy to report that he and his fellow prisoners were treated very kindly in Switzerland.

On their return to Earlston, each man received £5 from the Prisoners' Funds Committee.

As early as 1917 there were calls to establish a national war memorial. In October 1918, the Secretary for Scotland announced the composition of a Scottish War Memorial Committee, with Edinburgh Castle as the preferred site. However, in cities, towns and villages, there was a growing desire for local war memorials.

In Earlston, the first meeting to discuss the village memorial was scheduled to take place in late December 1918. A local paper reported that the meeting, 'Was to have been held at the Corn Exchange on Friday night to consider the erection of a war memorial, but only two or three ladies attended, and nothing was done'.[69]

Chapter 7

Social Change

The impact of the war on social change in terms of women's role in society and universal suffrage cannot be overstated.

In pre-war Earlston there were three main sources of employment open to women: the tweed mill, farm servant and domestic servant. Earlston is located in a rich agricultural area with many farms. Farming at that time, before the mechanization brought about by the war, was labour-intensive. Male farm servants (and hinds) were employed as ploughmen, who looked after the heavy horses. Unlike a modern tractor that might need to be fuelled once a day, heavy horses had to be rested for around two hours in the middle of the day. This was not time off for the ploughmen. Instead, they had to feed, water and groom their horse, in readiness for the afternoon's work. When the day's work was done – usually when it became too dark to continue – the ploughman would again tend to his horse and polish and repair its harness.

With the men engaged in looking after the horses, female farm servants were essentially labourers. As a consequence, men commanded a higher wage than women, and when the children of farm servants left school at fourteen years old, the eldest daughter was expected to go into domestic service. Which enabled the eldest son to remain at home and work on the farm, thus contributing to the household budget. This arrangement meant that domestic servants were cheap labour and so many more families could afford at least one live-in servant. The 1911 Government census showed that doctors, bank managers, solicitors and shop owners invariably had one or more servant.

There were many women's organizations that existed before 1914, and the war allowed them to expand and demonstrate women's contribution. Among these organizations were: Queen Alexandria's Imperial Military Nursing Service; First Aid Nursing Yeomanry; Territorial Force Nursing Service; Women's Hospital Corps (another hospital staffed entirely by women, initially rejected by the authorities just as Dr Inglis's had been); The Women's Volunteer Reserve; Women's Auxiliary Force; The Women's Legion; Women's Land Army; Almeric Paget Military Massage Corps (this Corps provided an early form of physiotherapy); Women's Forage Corps; Women's Forestry Corps; the Women's Royal Air Force (formed in 1918); and the Volunteer Aid Detachment.

In April 1917 the Volunteer Aid Detachment published an appeal in the *Southern Reporter*:

> Wanted, urgently wanted, more 'VADs.' The appeal that has just been issued springs from genuine and pressing need; and, if there are still any healthy, well-educated women between 17 and 50 who are wondering what they can do for their country, here is the answer.
>
> We talk of 'a VAD' for short, when what we mean is member of Voluntary Aid Detachment, formed under the Voluntary Aid Organization established by the War Office (on a scheme laid down by Sir Alfred Keogh) in 1909, with a special end in view; to fill the gap in the Territorial Medical

Service between the clearing hospital and the base in case of invasion. During the five years before the war, a number of women worked very hard, careless of a good deal of patronizing ridicule, to fit themselves for this particular work. They drilled, they learned theoretical and practical nursing, sanitation, cooking, odd jobs general. They learned to obey orders, to be cheerful under discomfort, and, when they could not get what they wanted, to make the best of what they had. Thus when the war came, they were ready; and it was not long before they were called upon to work which had never been contemplated in the original scheme. The organization was there; recruits flocked it in thousands; and now the once decried body is doing very various, invaluable work not only at home but in France and wherever there is a British Army.

It is all work for the sick and wounded, or for those who are working for the sick and wounded. Protected by the Red Cross under the Geneva Convention, they are careful to observe the limits imposed their neutrality. But within those limits, they do a vast quantity of things. Their auxiliary hospitals provide some 50,000 beds to the War Office, at an expense much smaller than that of the larger military hospitals. In the military hospitals, they help the nurses and take the places of men orderlies, dispensers, cooks, clerks, storekeepers. Under the Joint Committee of the British Red Cross Society and the Order of St John, they work the lines of communication and at the bases in France. Here they are to be found at the aid posts, feeding and tending the slightly wounded man on his way to the base. They staff the nurses' clubs. At the rest stations, they put sick and tired men to bed for the few hours good sleep that may prevent a serious illness. If there is an accident on the line, away they go with their ambulance, surgical appliances, and food. They drive motor-ambulances and drive them, it is said, more carefully than the men, doing their own engine cleaning, running repairs and tire-changing. They conduct hostels for hospital staffs and for the relatives the wounded. They make furniture, provide libraries for ambulance trains, grow vegetables and flowers. They do all kinds of work, some of it very rough; yet through it all, they are proud of exercising on weary, sick, and lonely men the influence of their gracious womanhood.

At present, there are some 80,000 of these 'VADs', and the cry goes up for thousands more. Those who may have volunteered already and been disappointed at not being needed at once will find that they are needed now when the spring activity has begun. They are needed at home, in France, in Malta, Egypt, Salonica. They are needed for unpaid daily in the VAD auxiliary hospitals at home. They are needed for nursing on general service in the military hospitals, where those who cannot work without pay are paid for by the War Office. They are needed in France for the various kinds of work under the Red Cross and the Order of St John—unpaid work, in this case because the organization does not wish divert a penny of the Joint Committee's funds from their proper object, the sick and wounded fighting men. Experienced women are needed to act as officers in charge of hostels. Motor-drivers are needed. Cooks (paid) are needed for the Near East. There is nothing that a woman can do, will learn to do, that does not come in useful. The work is hard. It for steadiness, cheerfulness, devotion, loyalty and discipline. But it is woman's work, noble in character, and of immense importance to the Empire; and no woman but might be justly proud of belonging to a body with such tradition and such a record of achievement as has this.[70]

This appeal was brutally frank in what a woman could expect if she chose to enlist. Whether this matter-of-fact style was successful is not known.

It would wrong to think that because they did not serve in combat roles the women were out of harm's way. The Commonwealth War Graves Commission lists the names of 165 women, who died in the service with the Volunteer Aid Detachment. Like their male counterparts, the volunteers were from all over the world: Canada, New Zealand, South Africa. They are buried in war cemeteries in Russia, Serbia, Italy, France and Egypt. One thing that is noticeable is the age range of the women that died compared to the men. The youngest VAD listed is just 16 years old, the oldest 67. Whereas the cause of death is not given, many succumbed to disease, including cerebrospinal meningitis, tuberculosis, septic poisoning due to contact with infected wounds, and also to flu during the pandemic. Others suffered a more violent death. Robert White's ship was torpedoed on the first day of 1917, and on the last day of the year the SS *Osmanieh*, en route to Alexandria, struck a mine and sank with the loss of 199 lives, including 8 VAD nurses. They are buried in the Alexandria (Hadra) War Cemetery.

Records show that there were several VAD volunteers from Berwickshire. Mary Barbara MacGregor worked as a VAD nursing sister at King George's Hospital, in London (Figure 20). Barbara, as this appears to be the name she preferred, was born in Suva, Fiji, in 1887, where her father, Sir William MacGregor, was Governor. Sir

William held a number of positions in the Colonial Service, including Governor of Queensland, and he was the first Chancellor of the University of Queensland. In 1914, Sir William retired to Chapel-on-Leader in Earlston, returning to Great Britain onboard the SS *Marathon* and arriving in London on 5 September 1914. Barbara died in London on 12 December 1934.

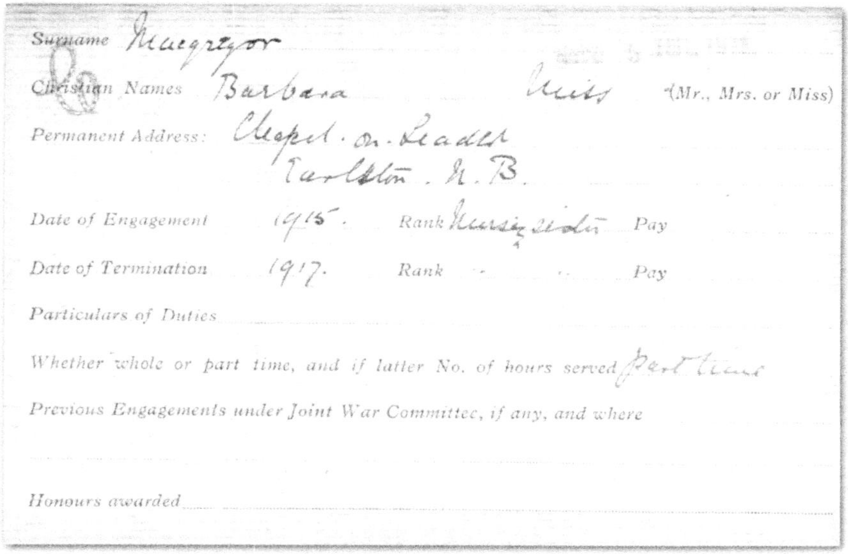
Surname Macgregor
Christian Names Barbara Miss (Mr., Mrs. or Miss)
Permanent Address: Chapel-on-Leader
Earlston. N.B.
Date of Engagement 1915. Rank Nursing sister Pay
Date of Termination 1917. Rank Pay
Particulars of Duties
Whether whole or part time, and if latter No. of hours served Part time
Previous Engagements under Joint War Committee, if any, and where
Honours awarded

Figure 20. Volunteer Aid Detachment Registration Card for Barbara MacGregor (Source: British Red Cross)

Other women from Berwickshire served locally, such as Margaret Veitch from Duns, who worked at Thirlestane Castle Auxiliary Hospital (Officers) in Lauder. Others served abroad: Jane Doughty from Ayton served in Egypt; Ellen Little from Coldstream worked as a chauffeuse in France; Annie Reid from Eccles served in Macedonia; and Grace Veitch from Duns served in Salonica. Men also served as orderlies with the VAD, such as Alexander Grierson, from the Schoolhouse in St Boswells.

In 1914, the military authorities failed to appreciate the contribution women could make to the war effort, but this attitude changed in 1916 with the publication of *Women's War Work*. By 1917, the attrition rate for soldiers was so high that the authorities were forced to acknowledge that it had to allow women to join the army and serve in France and Flanders, albeit not in combat roles.

Consequently, in 1917, the War Office announced the formation of the Women's Auxiliary Army Corps (WAAC), which would grow to about 57,000 women by the end of the war. Members took over positions previously held by men, such as cooks, drivers and clerks, freeing the men to take up front-line duties. Military prejudices and pettiness persisted. For example, the military refused to accept women as officers. Instead, they were given ranks such as controllers and administrators.

By December, the Government was recruiting women in a more traditional way – the Situations Vacant columns in newspapers. The Christmas Day edition of the *Berwickshire News and General Advertiser* carried the following advertisements:

> WAITRESSES, Experienced, WANTED, for Women's Auxiliary Army Corps to serve at home and overseas: £26 per annum all found: Uniform provided. ...
>
> DOMESTIC WORKERS WANTED, for Women's Auxiliary Army Corps to serve at home and overseas: £20 per annum all found: Uniform provided. ...
>
> COOKS, Experienced, WANTED, urgently for Women's Auxiliary Army Corps to serve at home and overseas: £26 per annum all found: Uniform provided. ...[71]

A number of local women are known to have enlisted in the WAAC. Agnes Stewart, who was born in Ledgerwood and had worked as a cook for a Mr McIntosh, solicitor, and his family in Haddington, enlisted. Margaret Pringle from Gordon, a village some 5 miles from Earlston, had worked as a bondager and table maid before she enlisted. Margaret was posted to France to work in the depot bases at Rouen and Étaples. Jessie Simpson, from Fans Farm, served in the WAAC until her discharge, when she took up employment as a lady's maid at East Morriston, a farm about 3 miles from Earlston.

On 6 February 1918, the Representation of the People Act received royal assent.[72] This Act gave the right to vote to men aged 21 and over, whether or not they owned property, which had been the previous restriction, and to women aged 30 and over, who resided in a constituency, or occupied land or premises with a rateable value of £5 or more, or whose husband did. At the same time, the Act extended the local government franchise to include women aged 21 and over on the same terms as men. The previous legislation, The Third Reform Act of 1884, had given the right to vote to male homeowners over the age of 21, leaving about 40 per cent of the male population – and thus millions of soldiers – ineligible to vote.

The Act had been debated in both Houses of Parliament in 1917, and achieved cross-party support. However, not everyone supported the Bill. For example, in June 1917, Lord Charnwood held a meeting to protest against the proposed inclusion of women in the Representation of the People Bill. He is quoted as having said that: 'the attempt made by a few people in the House of Commons to give votes to women was very mean and unfair. It was,' he went on to say, 'a cowardly, monstrous and un-English thing that people should attempt to rush through in the dark without having the opinion of the greater part of the electorate, who were away winning the war, or of the women concerned.'

And yet the war had been the significant factor in bringing about the legislation, which in turn, brought about social changes, such as closing the gap between classes, and recognizing the contribution that women made, not only to the war effort but also to society in general. However, when the Home Secretary, George Cave, introduced the Act, it was from a male perspective:

> War by all classes of our countrymen has brought us nearer together, has opened men's eyes, and removed misunderstandings on all sides. It has made it, I think, impossible that ever again, at all events in the lifetime of the present generation, there should be a revival of all the old class feeling which is responsible for so much, and, among other things, for the exclusion for a period, of so many of our population from the class of electors. I think I need say no more to justify this extension of the franchise.

The Act saw the size of the electorate increase threefold, from 7.7 million to 21.4 million. Women accounted for about 43 per cent of the electorate. However, unlike men, who had the right to vote if they were aged 21 or over, women had to be 30 years old. The age restriction was designed to ensure that women did not become the majority of the electorate, such had been the loss of men during the war. It would be another decade before women were granted the same voting rights as men.

For such a momentous change to the parliamentary system in Great Britain, it received very little press coverage: the *Scotsman*, for example, covered the event on page 5, with an article on Irish potatoes given precedence.[73]

Prior to the war, the last British General Election had been held in 1911, and with the coming of peace, it was time to plan for another. The Government had introduced new legislation, the Qualification of Women Act 1918, which received royal assent on 21 November, which gave women the right to stand in a general election. It is probably the shortest piece of law to be passed by Parliament, consisting of only twenty-seven operative words: 'A woman shall not be disqualified by sex or marriage for being elected to or sitting or voting as a Member of the Commons House of Parliament'. The law applied to women of 21 years and older.

In Earlston, the MP for Berwickshire, the Right Honourable H.J. Tennant, held a public meeting to address electors on Wednesday, 27 November. in the Corn Exchange.

In September a Labour candidate, Robert Fowlis, had held a public meeting in the Market Place. At the end of his speech, Fowlis had invited questions. However, as the *Southern Reporter* newspaper put it, he 'failed to meet with any serious response'.[74]

The election, which was held in December, saw John Hope, who had been the Liberal MP for Haddingtonshire, returned as the MP for the new Berwickshire and Haddingtonshire constituency. Fowlis gained 30 per cent of the vote. whereas Tennant, despite his previous Cabinet positions, achieved 16 per cent.

Thus the 1918 General Election was a first in many ways: the first election where all men had the right to vote; the first election where women over 30 years had the right to vote; and the first elected female Member of Parliament – Sinn Féin's Constance Markievicz, who refused to take up her seat in line with party policy.

Chapter 8

The War Memorial

On Auld Year's Night 1918, the traditional celebration at the Corn Exchange was enjoyed by around 100 couples dancing to music provided by Mr Robert Brown (violin), his daughter (piano) from St Boswells and Mr Adam Hewitt (cornet), an Earlstonian. With a break for first footin', the dance came to an end at around 4 a.m.

The event raised money for the Discharged Soldiers and Sailors Society, and many of the men who were present were in uniform. Recently returned to the village were Captain Smith and Lieutenant Brownlie (KOSB). Samuel Fisher's eldest son George was home from the Royal Navy, where he was serving as a sub-lieutenant in the Royal Navy Reserve, and George's brother, William, was starting his journey back to Earlston from a POW camp. Other men included H. Aikman (HLI), Air Mechanics T. Morris and A.S. Morris (RAF), Scott Donaldson (ASC), Private Fox (Royal Scots) and Sergeant Major T.D. Smith.

The *Berwickshire News and General Advertiser* reported that Captain Mitchell had presented one ton of coal to each of his estate workers as a Christmas gift; a very generous gift considering that coal was still rationed.[75]

Some businesses took advantage of the war effort and rationing to promote their products. A laundry soap manufacturer advertised its product on the grounds that it benefited the nation: 'Rinso – The cold-water washer – Save coal'. Other adverts reflected the changes the war had brought about. Although before the war, horses had been the primary source of power on farms, they were now being replaced by tractors. A local agricultural engineering company, Croall and Croall, advertised the availability of spares for Fordson farm tractors at their premises in St Boswells and Hawick.

On the evening of Sunday, 5 January 1919, a service was held to commemorate the lives of the soldiers who had died during the war. Mr Davidson, the church elder, read the names and ranks of the men, acknowledging which men were missing presumed dead, or men who were still missing. One man, Robert Wilson, who is commemorated on the war memorial, was still alive when the service was held.

In the early 1890s, Robert's mother, Helen Wilson, was employed as a domestic servant by a farmer in Redpath, some 2 miles from Earlston. Robert was born in 1895, but his place of birth is a mystery. It is given in various documents as Midlothian, Edinburgh (which is in Midlothian), and Morningside, an affluent suburb of Edinburgh. Morningside had several charitable institutions that offered care and help to 'fallen women', so perhaps Robert was illegitimate. There are no records of his birth in the statutory registers. Indeed, when Helen married in November 1910, her married status was shown as a spinster. Robert continued to use his mother's maiden name even after the birth of his half-sister, Mary Jane Hush, in February 1911.

By 1900, Robert was living with his grandmother in Smailholm, a small village about 5 miles from Earlston. Robert's mother was working as a domestic servant in St George, Edinburgh, before returning to Earlston parish sometime before 1910 and her marriage to Alexander Hush. The itinerant life continued, with the family moving to Craigsford Farm near Melrose, then St Boswells, which was given as Robert's place of residence on his Attestation Paper dated 8 September 1915. Robert enlisted in the Lothian and Border Horse regiment, however, on the top of the form, there is a handwritten note that shows that Robert's service number was P12051 and the Corps was MMP. The service number prefix 'P' indicates 'police' and 'MMP' was the abbreviation for the Mounted Military Police. Robert's death is recorded on the 'Return of Warrant Officers, Non-Commissioned Officers and Men for the Corps of Mounted Military Police Killed in Action', which lists Robert's age, place of birth, date and place of death, and cause of death.

Robert's date of death is 28 February 1919, in France, and the cause of death is pneumonia (possibly another victim of the Spanish Flu pandemic). In the Pension Records Ledger, Robert's entry has the additional information that the place of death was 44 CCS – No. 44 Casualty Clearing Station – which was located a few miles west of Ypres, at a place called Brandhoek, a small village between Poperinghe and Vlamertinghe, in Belgium, and not France, as entered in the ledger.

Although borders may have changed over the past 100 years, all the above points to the same Robert Wilson whose name is inscribed on the village war memorial. However, the Commonwealth War Graves Commission has Robert's grave listed as Cologne Southern Cemetery, in Nordrhein-Westfalen, Germany, hundreds of miles from Ypres, although there is no apparent reason why the army would choose to move a body such a distance.

Repatriated prisoners of war were becoming commonplace in the village. Many had experienced hardship during their captivity in Germany. One POW, however, had more pleasant memories. William Fisher, one of Samuel Fisher's four serving sons, was a corporal in the Royal Army Medical Corps. As he made his way back to Earlston, he recalled:

> We noticed the country becoming more mountainous for we were approaching the Alps. The panorama was one of the best, as the railway runs in and out among

the peaks. When one sits on the edge of the truck (we are granted this privilege) and views the magnificence of the Alpine scenery, with its grand majestic snow-capped peaks towering thousands of feet through the clouds beyond the range of human vision, like seats or thrones of great kings who might have inhabited the earth in the unknown past, one's earthly discomforts are completely forgotten, drive away by the awe-inspiring beauty of the Great Architect. One thing, in particular, would please father – the colour of the mountain streams. It is a beautiful transparent bluish-green caused by the melting snow. The effect is gorgeous, it dashes through the rocks, enshrouding the scene in a blue mist. These huge rocks are inhabited too. The houses are like a lot of white dots on the rocks. The effect, when illuminated at night, is also very fine. The people move up and down the mountain by means of pulley and car, like steeple-jacks. We had also a view of Mont Blanc. We afterwards passed through the longest tunnel in the world. There, electric power takes the place of steam, which would fill the tunnel with suffocating smoke.

In mid-January 1919, and perhaps embarrassed by the poor turnout at the December meeting, the Secretary of the Men's Committee, John Weatherston, called a meeting to discuss how to provide a war memorial. At the meeting, under the chairmanship of John Neil, a motion by Colonel Hope was carried – that a large committee would be appointed to consider the matter. And the committee was certainly large, with thirty-seven members. Colonel Hope was the chairman, Dodds, the bank manager, was the treasurer, the Reverend Davidson represented the church and George Dove, as the Mellerstain Estate Factor, represented the Earl of Haddington.

Only seven of the dead were represented by family members, and only one member of the committee, Bill Frater, had seen active service.

Within a month of that meeting, the committee considered a proposed design that would incorporate a Runic Cross with the names of the dead inscribed around the base. This design was deemed acceptable by the majority of the committee, and, more importantly, by Lady Binning of Mellerstain. Lady Binning vetoed the suggestion that the memorial be erected in the square opposite the Corn Exchange and indicated that she would accept the memorial being sited on the Green. And so, without any apparent sense of irony, the memorial to commemorate victory at the Battle of Waterloo was demolished to erect a monument to another war (see Figure 21).

Captain Mitchell told the committee that some places had decided to build cottages in memory of the fallen, which were to be given to the severely wounded, but this concept was not progressed. The Veterans Housing Association had been formed in 1915, but it would not be until after the Second World War that Earlston would provide two houses on Mill Road for veterans under this scheme.

It was agreed that a public meeting be held on 5 March to 'settle the question' regarding the final design.

Figure 21. Earlston Market Place showing the water pump and horse trough erected to commemorate the victory at the Battle of Waterloo.

On the last Wednesday in February, Earlston school children were given a half-day holiday, owing to a visit to the village of a 'Whippet' tank. The Scottish War Committee arranged visits to the towns and villages of Berwickshire as a token of thanks for their contribution to the war effort. Earlston had financed three larger tanks in response to the War Implements Investment Week, and this was an opportunity for villagers to see a tank, albeit a smaller, lighter version, up close. The tank trundled its way along the High Street from the east end of the village. It was notoriously difficult to control, but its two-man crew (on this occasion) managed to prevent it hitting anyone and made numerous stops so that curious adults and children could marvel at this war machine.

In late February, John Hardie, who had already lost one son in Gallipoli, received news from his daughter-in-law in Canada that his remaining son, James, had been killed at the Battle of Vimy, in September 1918. The report didn't come through official channels, but a soldier who was in the same platoon as James had informed his widow on his return to Canada.

A week later in early March, villagers found out that Robert Johnston had died in a German hospital, where he was being treated for his wounds following his capture.

A brief announcement of the War Memorial Committee meeting was reported in the *Scotsman* on 13 March, which read: 'Earlston – It has been decided to erect on the West Green, Earlston, a Runic or Ionic cross as the memorial to the local men who have fallen in the War'.[76] However, the final design did not have the agreement of the entire committee, as suggested in the *Scotsman*.

When the committee met in mid-April the chairman, Colonel Hope, tabled the minutes of the previous meeting, which reported that it had been decided that, 'Under all the circumstances the best memorial that could be erected would be a Northumbrian or Early

Christian Cross'. However, the vice-chairman, Mr J.M.D. Simpson, advised the committee that he had agreed to the cross design on his understanding that a bronze figure or statue would be too expensive, but had learned post-meeting that the cost was not nearly as much as he had been told.

Despite this new information, Colonel Hope proposed that a cross be erected, which was seconded by Mr Aitkenhead. Mr John Weatherston made a countermotion and proposed that a figure, rather than a cross be erected, provided the necessary funds could be raised. Mr W. Frater seconded this countermotion, and the motion was carried. The committee agreed to invite Mr Thomas Clapperton, a well-known local sculptor, to the next meeting to offer advice.

Clapperton was born in Galashiels in 1879, and studied at Galashiels Mechanics Institute before winning a scholarship to study at Glasgow Art School. He also studied at Kennington School of Art in London and the Royal Academy Schools. By the time he was invited to speak to the War Memorial Committee, he had been commissioned to design the Flodden Memorial at Braxton and the Mungo Park Memorial in Selkirk. Arguably his two most viewed works are the Robert the Bruce statue mounted on the wall at the entrance to Edinburgh Castle, and a frieze on the Liberty Building in London.

At his meeting with the committee in late April, Clapperton outlined his vision for the memorial, which would consist of the figure of a soldier in uniform. The statue would be cast in bronze and stand about six feet six inches high. The memorial would have a granite base on which bronze panels, inscribed with the name of the dead, would be mounted.

We can only assume that the committee gave Clapperton the go-ahead to finalize his design and the final cost.

In August 1919, the committee announced that it intended to raise £2,000 (equivalent to approx. £58,000 in 2019) to erect the memorial. Funds would be raised by voluntary subscriptions and not by entertainment, which was in contrast with the fundraising events for the war effort. Contributions could be made either as single sums or as instalments.

Tom Murdison, a committee member, was so passionate that a fitting memorial be erected that he felt compelled to compose an appeal to Earlstonians:

To Earlston Natives at Home and Abroad

For the sake of the auld hame, and bygone days and tender memories, may I ask if you can kindly help us with our War Memorial Scheme. We are desirous that every Earlstonian – near and far – might have the opportunist of remembering his or her native village in this fashion. Better there could not be. The brave boys (48 in number) who gave their all for us, were our and your successors here - laddies who, like many of us, in the long ago, played about the street of the old place, who spent many a glorious hour 'paddling' in the burn and the Leader, speeling' the Black Hill, picking' the berries, the room and the wild rose on our bonnie banks and braes, bird nesting' in the charming woods of Carolside and Cowdenknowes or kicking' the ba' on the Green around the old pump well.' For their sakes, and also to enable us to record their immortal names on imperishable bronze through out the ages, we shall gladly welcome whet you care to send us. with sincerest greetings from Leaderside, about which our local weaver-poet, the late James Sanderson, wrote nearly 80 years ago:

> O'er pebbly beds, by wooded banks,
> The Leader rushes on,

> By Rhymer's Tower and Blaikie's grave
> That tell of time long ago.
> To me more dear these sylvan shades,
> Than rivers more renowned.
> Loved memories linger on thy banks
> As on enchanted ground.[77]

Murdison planned that every house in Earlston should receive a copy of the appeal, but how he intended to supply Earlstonians 'living abroad' is not known.

Sadly, his appeal and other fundraising efforts failed to reach the £2,000 target. And so, instead of Clapperton's bronze statue, his more modest Celtic cross design was built (Figure 22). The memorial was described as a:

> Celtic Cross, with interlacing bands on all four sides, executed in Freetown granite, and stands on a rustic granite base in which are fixed three bronze panels bearing the names of the fallen and on the front the following dedicatory inscription: 'To the Glory of God and in memory of 48 men of the Parish of Earlston who gave their lives for King and Country during the Great War, 1914–1918. Their name liveth for evermore'.

The work was executed by Messrs G. Sutherland and Sons of Galashiels, at a total cost of £650.

It would be natural to assume that the names of the dead inscribed on the memorial were from Earlston parish, or at least have some family connection with the village, but that isn't necessarily the case.

A Village at War

Figure 22. Earlston War Memorial.

As mentioned earlier, a service of commemoration was held in the village church in January when the Reverend Walter Davidson conducted the devotional part of the service and the Reverend James Turner preached the sermon. The names of the fallen were read out. Comparing those names with those inscribed on the memorial we find that Privates James Dunn, Thomas Blackie, Robert Anderson and William Bell are not listed on the memorial.

Thomas Blackie was born in Earlston, but his name appears on the Hawick memorial; William Bell's father lived in a cottage at Town

Farm in Earlston yet his name is recorded on Lilliesleaf memorial, as is Robert Anderson, who lived and worked in Redpath, a village less than 2 miles from Earlston. Thomas Faichney, whose parents lived in Hawick, is listed on the memorial. Robert Halliday, whose mother lived at Bridgehaugh Mill, Earlston, is listed neither on the memorial nor was mentioned during the service. Lance Corporal James Rogers, whose wife lived in Earlston, was similarly absent from the service list and the memorial.

It is sobering to consider that the number of war dead from a small village might well exceed the forty-eight men recorded on the memorial.

Although the War Memorial Committee continued to argue over what was 'the best' tribute to Earlston's dead, a peace celebration was held in July 1919, which took the form of a picnic on the banks of the Leader River, close to Cowdenknowes House, home of Colonel and Mrs Hope. A sports day was held in a field at Sorrowlesfield Farm on the other side of the river, connected by bridge to the picnic site. That evening a beacon was lit on the summit of the Blackhill and a firework display was held.

Newspaper coverage of the event suggested that it was very well supported. The reports include the names of the successful athletes in the family sports events. Few, if any, of those watching the children run their races would have imagined that in twenty years' time that generation would also be ordered to fight another war.

Two years later, on the afternoon of 13 November 1921, the unveiling ceremony of the war memorial took place (Figure 23). A sizeable crowd gathered for the occasion, with the ceremony presided over by Colonel Hope (Figure 24). Before asking his wife to unveil the memorial, he addressed the crowd. His speech concluded:

This memorial cross which we are about to unveil will keep the memories of these brave men always before the minds of those seeing it from day to day or passing by it from time to time. We are proud also to see present today so many of those gallant men who went forth from this parish and have been spared to return to their homes. And now having all pulled together to win the war – for I really think that those who had to stay at home did something to help – shall we not all pull together to win the true peace and prosperity which are so much wanted throughout the world after all the devastations of the war.

> # The Earlston War Memorial.
> ## Unveiling Ceremony
> By Colonel and Mrs Hope of Cowdenknowes,
> **SUNDAY, 13th NOVEMBER, 1921, at 3 p.m.**
> CHAIRMAN. — J. M. D. SIMPSON, Esq.
>
> "*They shall not grow old as those who are left grow old,
> Age shall not weary, nor the years contemn:
> At the going down of the sun and in the morning,
> We shall remember them.*"

Figure 23. Earlston War Memorial unveiling ceremony programme.

Figure 24. Crowds attending the unveiling ceremony.

The clock was ticking on world peace.

1921 saw the unveiling of the Earlston war memorial, the creation of the Royal British Legion and the adoption of the poppy as a symbol of remembrance.

In 1915, a Canadian doctor, Lieutenant Colonel John McCrae was stationed at the Essex Farm Advanced Dressing Station near Ypres (Figure 25). His close friend, Alexis Helmer, had been killed in battle on 2 May, and McCrae conducted his burial service. McCrae noted how quickly the poppies grew around the graves and the following day, sitting in the back of a field ambulance, he composed his seminal poem 'In Flanders' Field'.

The poem's opening verse presents the reader with the image of a landscape of chaos and destruction, with row upon orderly row of graves and thousands of delicate poppies growing between the graves and shell craters.

Figure 25. Essex Farm Advanced Dressing Station photographed in 2018.

The poem inspired American Moina Michael to make and sell red silk poppies, some of which were brought to England by a French woman, Anna Guérin.

The fledgling Royal British Legion adopted the poppy as a symbol of remembrance and started producing them to raise funds, by selling them each year for Remembrance Day. Such was their popularity that only a few of these poppies were available in Scotland.

Lady Haig, wife of Field Marshall Haig, whose ancestral home was at Bemersyde about 4 miles from Earlston, established the Lady Haig Poppy Factory outside Edinburgh in 1926. Lady Haig insisted that the poppies made at the factory were botanically correct and so all poppies manufactured in Scotland have four petals and no leaf, unlike those produced elsewhere, which have two petals and a leaf.

On Monday, 8 August 1922, the War Memorial Committee held its last meeting in the parish church hall.[78] With Colonel Hope of Cowdenknowes presiding, the accounts relative to the memorial were examined and found to be correct, with a balance of 13s 10d in hand.

After reading the War Memorial Committee reports and the passion of Tom Murdison's appeal for funds, one wonders if, when the memorial was finally unveiled, the expectations of the families of the dead, the survivors and other villagers had been met. Clapperton's designs for the Selkirk and Canonbie war memorials were unveiled before Earlston's. Were those designs, which incorporated statues similar to his original proposal, more in keeping with what Earlstonians had thought would be 'the best' tribute? We will never know.

Chapter 9

United States of Europe

At the outset of this book, I wanted to discover something about the men whose names are inscribed on the war memorial. I was convinced that each had a story to tell, and that there would be something unique that would make him all the more memorable. Hopefully, I have achieved that.

I also wanted to convey an idea of the scale of the loss to the village. The Roll of Honour (Appendix 1) lists the names of the men who died, the names of their parents and, where applicable, those of their siblings, wife and children. The list reveals that the deaths of the 48 men touched almost 300 immediate family members. Every man, woman and child in the village would have known at least one of the dead.

How the villagers were affected by the slaughter brought about by this new, industrialized warfare was captured by that Earlston worthy, Tom Murdison. In February 1915, with the war barely six months old, Tom, an apparent believer in the power of poetry, penned his poem 'The Great War'. In describing the nightmarish events unfolding across Europe, he wrote in his native Lallans:

> Sic' horror, terror, death – 'tis shameful
> To read it, far less see'd – 'tis painful.
> Who ever thocht, wi a' oor lear,
> In nineteen hunner' and fifteen year,
> There would be bloodshed,
> loss o' life Wi' millions crippled in the strife;
> Who ever thocht we'd live to see,
> Sic terrifying butchery; –

Despite the loss and the butchery, it says much about the character of Earlston that, in 1919, the village chose to celebrate peace, not victory. And in 1945, the village chose to celebrate the safe return of the villagers who had served – not victory in Europe.

In 1919, Captain Balfour, KOSB, acquired six German guns as 'war trophies'.[79] One gun was given to Earlston and placed on the West Green. No doubt the 'trophy' had some novelty value, but that soon wore off. After, it only served as an unwanted reminder of times the villagers would rather forget. Things came to a head in 1921 when, a week before the new war memorial was scheduled to be unveiled, the Earlston branch of the Royal British Legion wrote to the Parish Council.[80] The letter stated that the ex-servicemen of Earlston took strong objection to the gun being in such proximity to the memorial and requested that the council have it removed. The request was complied with before the unveiling ceremony took place.

The First World War was fought to stop the spread of extreme nationalism in Europe. When the Armistice was signed in 1918, world leaders recognized that something had to be done to prevent future wars. And so, in 1920, at the Paris Peace Conference, the League of Nations was formed. Its mission was world peace and its primary goals included preventing wars through collective security and disarmament, and settling international disputes through negotiation and arbitration.

The organization's mission failed spectacularly in 1939, with the outbreak of the Second World War. At the end of that war, an alternative means for European peace was sought.

The solution had been identified 100 years earlier by Victor Hugo, the French novelist. At the International Peace Conference, held in Paris in 1849, Hugo stated he favoured the creation of, 'A supreme, sovereign senate, which will be to Europe what Parliament is to England'. He went on to say: 'A day will come when all nations on our continent will form a European brotherhood … A day will come when we shall see … the United States of America and the United States of Europe face to face, reaching out for each other across the seas'[81].

This vision of a United States of Europe was voiced by Mikhail Bakunin at the 1867 League for Peace and Freedom in Geneva. Bakunin stated that:

> In order to achieve the triumph of liberty, justice and peace in the international relations of Europe, and to render civil war impossible among the various peoples which make up the European family, only a single course lies open: to constitute the United States of Europe.

In the aftermath of the Second World War, six European countries created the European Coal and Steel Community (ECSC).

French Foreign Minister Robert Schuman first proposed the ECSC on 9 May 1950, as a way to prevent further war between France and Germany. He declared that he aimed to, 'Make war not only unthinkable but materially impossible', which was to be achieved by regional integration, of which the ECSC was the first step.

The ECSC was formally established by the Treaty of Paris, signed by Belgium, France, Italy, Luxembourg, the Netherlands and West Germany.

The Treaty created a common market for coal and steel among its member states, which served to neutralize competition between European nations over natural resources, particularly steel-making in Germany and coal mining in Belgium and France.

The ECSC was the first international organization to be based on the principles of supranationalism, to regulate industrial production under a centralized authority and start the process of formal integration, which ultimately led to the European Union.

From the ECSC to the European Economic Community to the European Union, the model of economic interdependency has proved successful, 'to make wars not only unthinkable but materially impossible'.

As a consequence, the member states of the EU have enjoyed their longest period of peace and prosperity.

In 2016, the British Government held a referendum to ask the electorate if the UK should remain a member of the EU. The result was that a majority of the votes cast showed people were convinced that membership of the European Union was not in the best interest of the United Kingdom and so, in 2020, the UK left the EU.

What would the men named on Earlston war memorial conclude from this action? Would they have agreed with John McCrae in his poem, 'In Flanders Field', that the EU represented an opportunity to 'take up the quarrel with the foe', using words rather than guns and gas? Would they consider that having fought and died in good faith, their sacrifice was meaningful, but that by leaving the EU that faith had been broken?

Acknowledgements

I am indebted to Auld Earlston, a group of local amateur historians, for access to its extensive library of old photographs donated by residents. (Figures 2, 21, 23 and 24).

I must also thanks Sheila MacKay (Figures 10 and 18) and Laura MacKenzie (Figure 11) or sharing photographs from their family tree. Kathy Taylor shared her photo of the Essex Advanced Dressing Station (Figure 25) and the Australian War Memorial licenced the publication of Figures 7 and 8.

All other photo's are from my collection unless otherwise stated.

I want to express my thanks to my brother David, Kathy Batty, Secretary of Lord Strathcona's Horse (Royal Canadians), Brian Talty, MMM CD, and Marcel Chenier, MMM CD, Canadian Armed Forces for their hospitality and military knowledge during my 2018 visit to the Menin Gate and Moreuil Wood.

Gale Winskill of Winskill Editorial deserves a mention. Gale provided invaluable insight and help through her critique of my manuscript and proofreading the final document.

And finally, I want to thank my daughters, Rachel and Rebecca, for their support and encouragement.

Jeff Price
April 2021

Endnotes

1. *Southern Reporter*, 'Earlston', 15 February 1917, p.5.
2. Alchin, W. (1980), *As I recall: Childhood Memories of Newstead*, Weekender Graphics.
3. *Berwick Advertiser*, 'Earlston and the War', 14 August 1914, p.5.
4. *Ibid*.
5. *Berwick Advertiser*, 'Price of Wales National Relief Fund War', 21 August 1914, p.5.
6. *Berwick Advertiser*, 'Great Public Meeting', 21 August 1914, p.5.
7. *Edinburgh Evening News*, 'Recruiting in Country Districts: Are the Hinds hanging back?' 21 October 1914, p.4.
8. *Berwick Advertiser*, 'Route March of the 4th K.O.S.B.', 6 November 1914, p.5.
9. *Ibid*.
10. *Berwick Advertiser*, 'Northern Cyclists Reserve Battalion', 9 October 1914, p.5.
11. *Berwick Advertiser*, 'The Hartlepool Bombardment: An Earlston Man's Experience', 1 January 1915, p.5.
12. *Berwick Advertiser*, 'The Death of Private James Archibald K.O.S.B.', 26 February 1915, p.8.
13. *Jedburgh Gazette*, 'German Barbarism', 21 May 1915, p.3.
14. *Berwick Advertiser*, 'Earlston', 12 February 1915, p.7.
15. Gillon, Captain Stair (2002; originally published 1930), *The K.O.S.B. in the Great War*, Naval and Military Press.

16. The Long, Long Trail: Researching soldiers of the British Army in the Great War of 1914–1919, 'The Battle of Aubers'. Available at: http://www.longlongtrail.co.uk/battles/battles-of-the-western-front-in-france-and-flanders/the-battle-of-aubers/ (accessed June 2020).
17. *Berwick Advertiser*, 'Recruiting Tour by Caravan', 7 May 1915, p.3.
18. *Berwickshire News and General Advertiser*, 'Our Third Roll of Honour: Berwick and Berwickshire Patriots', 28 December 1915, p.4.
19. *War Diary 52 Division 155 Brigade 1/4 King's Own Scottish Borders 1915 June–1916 January*, National Archive, pp. 5f.
20. *Southern Reporter*, 'Pathetic Letter', 13 January 1916, p.5.
21. *War Diary, Op. cit.*
22. *Berwick Advertiser*, 'Earlston Sergeant's interesting Letter', 13 August 1915, p.5.
23. *Southern Reporter*, 'Border Territorials at Gallipoli', 24 February 1916, p.4.
24. *Berwickshire News*, 'Earlston Man in Suvla Bay Landing', 16 November 1915, p.3.
25. *Berwickshire News*, 'Football on the Streets of Earlston' 16 February 1932, p.5.
26. *Berwick Advertiser*, 'The Berwick Tribunal', 29 June 1917, p.4.
27. *Berwickshire News*, 'County Tribunal', 21 March 1916, p.6.
28. *Ibid.*
29. *Berwick Advertiser*, 'County Tribunal', 24 March 1916, p.4.
30. *Women's War Work* (1916), London: War Office HMSO.
31. *Southern Reporter*, 'Border Notes and Comments', 9 March 1916, p.4.
32. *Southern Reporter*, 'Heavy Fines for Failing to obscure Lights', 20 April 1917, p.7.
33. *Hansard*, HC Deb, 10 August 1916, vol. 85, cc 1208–9.
34. *Southern Reporter*, 'Border News in Brief', 2 November 1916, p.6.

35. *Berwick Advertiser*, 'Earlston', 12 October 1917, p.12.
36. *Berwickshire News and General Advertiser*, 'St Abbs Boy drowned', 21 November 1916, p.3.
37. *Berwickshire News and General Advertiser*, 'Earlston Man missing', 17 October 1916, p2
38. *Berwickshire News and General Advertiser*, 'Earlston', 12 December 1916, p3
39. *Berwickshire News and General Advertiser*, 'In Memoriam', 18 September 1917, p3
40. *Berwick Advertiser*, 'More Men from the Land', 19 January 1917, p2
41. *Berwickshire News and General Advertiser*, 'Earlston Casualties', 22 May 1917, p2
42. Gillon, *Op.cit.*, p.266.
43. *Southern Reporter*, 'Earlston Patriotism', 3 February 1916, p.5.
44. *Berwick Advertiser*, 'The Little Difference', 22 June 1917, p.4.
45. *Berwick Advertiser*, 'Berwick Military Tribunal', 30 November 1917, p.4.
46. *Southern Reporter*, 'Earlston Social', 12 April 1917, p.5.
47. *Southern Reporter*, 'Local Casualties', 15 November 1917, p.5.
48. *Berwickshire News and General Advertiser*, 'Earlston', 5 November 1918, p.3.
49. War Office Daily List No.5437, 8 December 1917, Archive Reference No. NLS 1917_WList19.
50. War Office Daily List No.5437, 20 December 1917, Archive Reference No. NLS 1917_WList21.
51. Weekly Casualty List, 'Missing: Northumberland Fusiliers', 11 December 1917 (War Office & Air Ministry), p.35.
52. *Berwickshire News and General Advertiser*, 'Earlston', 14 January 1919, p.3.
53. *War Diary 29th Division 86th Infantry Brigade 2 Battalion Royal Fusiliers*, Vol. 32, October 1917, National Archive.

54. The Long, Long Trail, 'Locations of British Casualty Clearing Stations'. Available at: https://www.longlongtrail.co.uk/army/regiments-and-corps/locations-of-british-casualty-clearing-stations/ (accessed June 2020).
55. *Southern Reporter*, 'Roll of Honour: Earlston', 17 May 1917, p.4.
56. *Berwickshire News and General Advertiser*, 'Earlston Men's War Guild Committee', 11 December 1917, p.2.
57. *Berwickshire News and General Advertiser*, 'On Farm and in Garden', 1 January 1918, p.7.
58. *The Meat (Maximum Prices) Order 1917* (No. 903).
59. *Daily Record*, 'Earlston's Big Gas Push', 14 June 1918, p.3.
60. *Berwickshire News and General Advertiser*, 'Price of gas by Earlston Gas Company', 11 June 1918, p.3.
61. *Berwickshire News and General Advertiser*, 'Berwickshire and Soldiers' Homes', 5 February 1918, p.3.
62. McCrae's Battalion Trust, 'The Sporting Battalion'. Available at: http://www.mccraesbattaliontrust.org.uk/the-sporting-battalion/ (accessed June 2020).
63. *Southern Reporter*, 'Board of Agriculture Scotland Military Service (No. 2) Act 1918: Notice to Farmers and Farm Workers', 2 May 1918, p.1.
64. *Hawick News and Border Chronicle*, 'Pte. Adam Wilson', 31 May 1918, p.4.
65. British Army WW1 Service Records, 1914–1920, Alexander Simpson, S/3647, National Archives.
66. Hutchinson, Lt-Col G.S., *Machine Guns: Their History and Tactical Employment* (2009), Naval and Military Press, p.115.
67. *Southern Reporter*, 'Death of Local Soldier', 1 August 1918, p.3.
68. *Southern Reporter*, 'Border Heroes', 14 November 1918, p.4.
69. *Southern Reporter*, 'Earlston War Memorial', 26 December 1918, p.7.
70. *Southern Reporter*, 'VAD: An Appeal to Women', 26 April 1917, p.3.

71. *Berwickshire News and General Advertiser*, 'Wanted', 25 December 1917, p.2.
72. Representation of the People Act (1918), Parliamentary Archives, HL/PO/PU/1/1918/7&8G5c64.
73. *Scotsman*, 'Irish Potatoes', 7 February 1918, p.5.
74. *Southern Reporter*, 'Political Meeting', 5 September 1918, p.3.
75. *Berwickshire News and General Advertiser*, 'Earlston', 7 January 1919, p.3.
76. *Scotsman*, 'Scottish War Memorials', 13 March 1919, p.4.
77. *Berwickshire News and General Advertiser*, 'Earlston Parish War Memorial', 12 August 1919, p.4.
78. *Berwickshire News and General Advertiser*, 'Earlston', 8 August 1922, p.7.
79. *Berwickshire News and General Advertiser*, 'War Trophies', 13 May 1919, p.6.
80. *Southern Reporter*, 'Earlston Parish Council', 3 November 1921, p.5.
81. *Sydney Morning Herald*, 'Speech of Victor Hugo to the Peace Congress in Paris', 26 December 1849, p.3.

Appendix 1

Roll of Honour

The following information has been compiled from records available from the Commonwealth War Graves Commission and Scotland's People.

Aikman, William Fairbairn, Sergeant, 1/4th King's Own Scottish Borderers
Service No.: 4371
Date Died: 12 July 1915
Aged: 25
Place of death: Achi Baba Nullah, Gallipoli
Remembered at: Helles Memorial
Son of: Henry & Lavinia Aikman, Brooklyn Cottage, Earlston
Sibling of: Henry (twin), John
Father of: David

Aitchison, Alexander S, Private, 18th Highland Light Infantry
Service No.: 41676
Formerly: King's Own Scottish Borderers, Service No. 27062
Date Died: 25 August 1917
Aged: 39

Place of death: Gillemont Farm
Remembered at: Thriepval Memorial
Son of: Alexander & Christine Aitchison, Lintlaw Cottages
Sibling of: Mary, Robert, Isabella, William
Husband of: Isabella Hunter
Father of: Annie Simpson, Margaret Forrest

Archibald, James Scott, Private, 4th King's Own Scottish Borderers
Service No.: 4455
Date Died: 14 February 1915
Age: 19
Place of death: At home
Remembered at: Earlston Parish Church Cemetery
Son of: James & Robina Archibald, High Street, Earlston
Sibling of: John, Thomas, Joan

Baillie Hamilton, George, Lord Binning, Brigadier General, Royal Horse Guards
Date Died: 12 January 1917
Aged: 60
Remembered at: Tyninghame Burial Ground, East Linton, East Midlothian, Scotland
Son of: George Baillie-Hamilton-Arden, 11th Earl of Haddington and Helen Katherine Warrender
Sibling of: Isabel, Ruth, Richard, Grisell, Henry, Cecily
Husband of: Katherine Augusta Millicent Salting
Father of: George, Helen O'Brien, Charles William

Ballantyne, David, Private, 7/8th King's Own Scottish Borderers
Service No.: 40239
Date Died: 15 September 1916
Aged: 19

Place of death: Martinpuich, Battle of Flers-Courcelette
Remembered at: Thiepval Memorial
Son of: Robert & Isabella Ballantyne, Thorn Street, Earlston
Sibling of: Ella

Black, Archibald, Private, 2nd King's Own Scottish Borderers
Service No.: 25281 King's Own Scottish Borderers
Second Service No.: 368496 Labour Corps
Date Died: 24 October 1918
Aged: 19
Place of death: Died of pneumonia in hospital in France.
Remembered at: Awoingt British Cemetery
Son of: Archibald & Alice Black, Station Road, Earlston
Sibling of: Alexander, Jane, Alice, Herriot, Jessie.

Borthwick, David Adam, 16th Battalion, 9th Royal Scots
Service No.: 352484
Date Died: 27 April 1918
Aged: 25
Place of death: War Hospital, Lille
Remembered at: Lille Southern Cemetery
Son of: Thomas & Janet Borthwick, Redpath, Melrose, Roxburghshire
Sibling of: Thomas, Robert, James, William, Agnes, Janet, Margaret

Boyd, John, Private, 1/4th Seaforth Highlanders
Service No.: 20311
Date Died: 24 July 1918
Aged: 20
Place of death: Battle of Marne
Remembered at: St Imoges Churchyard
Son of: Philip & Helen Boyd, 5 Roger's Place, Earlston.
Sibling of: Philip, Maggie, Ellen, Annie

Cessford, Alexander, Private, 1/4th King's Own Scottish Borderers
Service No.: 6748
Date Died: 12 July 1915
Age: 23
Place of death: Achi Baba Nullah, Gallipoli
Remembered at: Helles Memorial
Son of: William & Jane Cessford, Haughhead Buildings, Earlston
Sibling of: Mary, George, Alexander

Dickson, John, Private, 155th Company Machine Gun Corp
Service No.: 120532
Formerly: Scottish Borderers, Service No. 4522
Date Died: 8 November 1917
Age: 29
Place of death: Wadi el Hesi
Remembered at: Gaza War Cemetery
Son of: Alexander & Helen Dickson, Thorn Street, Earlston
Sibling of: George
Husband of: Agnes Jardine (née Douglas)
Father of: Alexander, James

Duff, Henry, Private, 15th Canadian Infantry
Service No.: 192423
Date Died: 27 September 1918
Aged: 23
Remembered at: Sains-Les-Marquion British Cemetery
Son of: Archibald & Helen Duff, High Street (Cottage in back court), Earlston
Sibling of: Jane, Annie, Nora, Isabel

Elliott, Henry, Private, 7/8th King's Own Scottish Borderers
Service No.: 29367
Date Died: 27 February 1917

Aged: 36
Place of death:
Remembered at: Habarcq Communal Cemetery Extension
Son of: Robert & Anne Elliot, Bedrule
Sibling of: Helen, Ann, Catherine, Robert, Thomas, Jane, Edward
Husband of: Catherine Wright Elliot (née Paxton), Scraesburgh, Jedburgh
Father of: Margaret Whitelaw

Faichney, Thomas, Private, 8/10th Gordon Highlanders
Service No.: 291473
Date Died: 26 August 1917
Aged: 35
Place of death: Passchendaele
Remembered at: Tyne Cot Memorial
Son of: Thomas and Mary Faichney, Hawick

Fairley, Alexander, Lance Corporal, 9th Battalion, Black Watch
Service No.: S/6576
Date Died: 25 September 1915
Aged: 25
Place of death: Battle of Loos
Remembered at: Philosophe British Cemetery, Mazingarbe
Son of: John and Jane Fairley, Westruther, Berwickshire
Sibling of: Susan

Forbes, Henry William, Sergeant, 16th Battalion Canadian Scottish
Service No.: 29518
Date Died: 27 April 1915
Aged: 35
Remembered at: Hazebrouck Communal Cemetery
Son of: Arthur & Mary A Forbes, Mellerstain, Gordon, Berwickshire
Sibling of: Christopher, Lizzie, Arthur

Gillie, Thomas, Lance Corporal, 12th Battalion Machine Gun Corps
Service No.: 33865
Date Died: 2 July 1918
Aged: 23
Place of death: Somme
Remembered at: Gezaincourt Communal Cemetery Extension
Son of: Thomas & Jessie Gillie, East End, Earlston
Sibling of: George

Graham, William, Private, Remount Depot, Army Service Corps
Service No.: R4/062384
Date Died: 6 July 1915
Aged: 36
Place of death: Alexandria
Remembered at: Alexandria (Chatby) Military and War Memorial Cemetery
Son of: William and Ellen Graham
Husband of: Annie Graham
Father of: Agnes, Winifred

Hardie, James, Company Sergeant Major, 1st Canadian Mounted Rifles
Service No.: 781117
Date Died: 14 September 1918
Aged: 39
Remembered at: Vimy Memorial
Son of: John & Charlotte Hardie, High Street, Earlston
Sibling of: Jane, Isabella, Joan, Betsy, John
Husband of: Janet Hardie, Manitoba St. East, Moose Jaw, Saskatchewan, Canada
Father of: Jemima

Hardie, John Thomas, Private, 1/4th King's Own Scottish Borderers
Service No.: 4539
Date Died: 12 July 1915
Age: 25
Place of death: Achi Baba Nullah, Gallipoli
Remembered at: Helles Memorial
Son of: John & Charlotte D Hardie, Thistle House, The Square, Earlston
Sibling of: Jane, Isabella, Joan, Betsy, James

Hewitt, John, Private, 1st/13th Kensington Battalion, London Regiment
Service No.: 2911
Date Died: 9 May 1915
Aged: 21
Place of death: Battle of Aubers
Remembered at: Ploegsteert Memorial
Son of: Adam & Agnes Hewitt, 11 Roger's Place, Earlston
Sibling of: Robert, James

Johnston, George Braidford, Private, 1/4th King's Own Scottish Borderers
Service No.: 7058
Date Died: 12 July 1915
Aged: 24
Place of death: Achi Baba Nullah, Gallipoli
Remembered at: Helles Memorial
Son of: George & Helen Johnston, Thorn Street, Earlston
Sibling of: John, Thompson, Isabella

Kerr, William, Private, 1st/6th Battalion, Seaforth Highlanders
Service No.: S/41896
Formerly: S/23773, Argyll and Sutherland Highlanders

Date Died: 12 October 1918
Aged: 19
Place of death:
Remembered at: Queant Communal Cemetery British Extension
Son of: William and Annie Kerr, West High Street, Earlston, Berwickshire
Sibling of: Jenny, James, Maggie and Alexander

Kerr, William James Grieve, Private, 4th Battalion, King's Own Scottish Borderers
Service No.: 7076
Date Died: 19 October 1915
Aged: 29
Place of death: 17th General Hospital Alexandria
Remembered at: Alexandria (Chatby) Military and War Memorial Cemetery
Son of: James & Rachel Kerr, Green View, Earlston
Sibling of: Jane, Euphemia, Thomas, Helen, Mary

Lees, Robert, Private, 1st Battalion King's Own Scottish Borderers
Service No.: 201585
Date Died:25 November 1917
Aged: 37
Place of death: Battle of Cambrai
Remembered at: Rocquigny-Equancourt Road British Cemetery, Manancourt
Son of: John and Margaret Lees
Sibling of: Maggie, William, Janet, George, Thomas
Husband of: Margaret Wilson Anthony

Lunam, David, Private, 13th Yorkshire Regiment
Service No.: 33855
Formerly: Army Service Corps, Service No. S/2/SR029

Date Died: 27 March 1918
Aged: 35
Place of death: Battle of Étaples
Remembered at: Étaples Military Cemetery
Son of: David and Isabella Lunan
Sibling of: Euphemia, Mary, Thomas

Milne, Alexander, Sergeant, 1st Battalion King's Own Scottish Borderers
Service No.: 9400
Date Died: 26 April 1915
Aged: 26
Place of death: Gallipoli
Remembered at: Helles Memorial
Son of: Malcolm and Henrietta (née Cormack)
Sibling of: William, Elizabeth, Isabella, Douglas, Katie

Notman, James, Private, 5th (Service) Battalion Cameron Highlanders
Service No.: S/18449
Date Died: 27 November 1915
Aged: 19
Place of death: Arras
Remembered at: Railway Dugouts Burial Ground (Transport Farm)
Son of: Alexander and Susan Notman

Paterson, David, Lance Corporal, Royal Canadian Regiment
Service No.: 477702
Date Died: 3 August 1916
Aged: 25
Remembered at: Menin Road South Military Cemetery
Son of: Stewart and Jane Paterson, Church Street, Earlston
Sibling of: Elizabeth, Helen

Robertson, James William, Lance Corporal, 16th Battalion Royal Scots
Service No.: 301786
Date Died: 21 March 1918
Aged: 36
Place of death: Battle of Arras
Remembered at: Arras Memorial
Son of: James and Agnes (née Norman) Robertson
Sibling of: Elizabeth, George, John
Husband of: Catherine Tully

Simpson, Alexander, Lance Corporal, 11th Battalion Argyll & Sutherland Highlanders
Service No.: S/3647
Date Died: 20 April 1918
Aged: 31
Place of death: Battle of Arras
Remembered at: Feuchy Chapel British Cemetery, Wancourt
Son of: Andrew and Helen (née Spence) Simpson
Sibling of: John, Jessie, Andrew, George, Robert, Elizabeth

Simpson, George, Private, 14th Highland Light Infantry
Service No.: 42842
Formerly: King's Own Scottish Borderers, Service No. 7743
Date Died: 29 July 1917
Aged: 25
Place of death: Gillemont Farm
Remembered at: Tincourt New British Cemetery
Son of: Alexander and Elizabeth Simpson
Sibling of: Euphemia, Jane

Slassor, Walter, Private, 1/4th Battalion Northumberland Fusiliers
Service No.: 203129
Date Died: 26 October 1917
Aged: 31
Place of death: Passchendaele
Remembered at: Tyne Cot Memorial
Son of: William and Margaret Slassor, Northumberland
Sibling of: Catherine, Isabella, Ursula, John, Mary
Husband of: Annie Slassor (née Scott), North Lodge Cottage, Blagdon, Seaton Burn

Steedman, A.H., Captain, 10th Battalion Scottish Rifles
Date Died: 30 March 1917
Aged: 30
Place of death: First Battle of the Scarpe
Remembered at: Duisans British Cemetery, Étrun
Son of: John and Isabella Steedman
Sibling of: Robert, John, Henry
Husband of: Winifred Theresa Steedman (née Beattie)
Father of: Jeanette Winifred

Stirling, William, Private, 6th Battalion Cameron Highlanders
Service No.: S/10299
Date Died: 25 September 1915
Aged: 20
Place of death: Battle of Loos
Remembered at: Loos Memorial
Son of: Charles and Marion (née Fisher) Stirling, Haughhead Road, Earlston
Sibling of: Christina, George, Hannah, Jessie, Charlotte, Mainie, Joseph, Edelyn, Edith, Maggie

Thomson, James, Private, 6th Battalion King's Own Scottish Borderers
Service No.: 12734
Date Died: 25 September 1915
Aged: 28
Place of death: Battle of Loos
Remembered at: Loos Memorial
Son of: John and Janet Martin
Note: Thomson's death was reported in The Southern Reporter on 28 October 1915 stating that he was also known as James Martin.

Todd, George, Private, 2nd King's Own Scottish Borderers
Service No.: 23777
Date Died: 4 October 1917
Aged: 38
Place of death: Passchendaele
Remembered at: Tyne Cot Memorial
Son of: Peter and Mary (née Crombie) Todd, Lambden, Greenlaw
Sibling of: Elizabeth
Husband of: Janet Todd (née Scott), 30 Bank Street, Cambuslang, Glasgow

Turnbull, Henry C, Private, 1/4th King's Own Scottish Borderers
Service No.: 4448
Date Died: 5 October 1916
Aged: 23
Place of death: Baghdad
Remembered at: Baghdad (North Gate) War Cemetery
Son of: James and Mary Turnbull, Lindean, Earlston
Sibling of: William, James, Mary

Turnbull, William, Private, 1/4th Battalion King's Own Scottish Borderers
Service No.: 6765
Date Died: 15 July 1915
Aged: 29
Place of death: Achi Baba Nullah, Gallipoli
Remembered at: Lancashire Landing Cemetery
Son of: James and Mary Turnbull, Lindean, Earlston
Sibling of: Henry, James, Mary
Husband of: Elizabeth Anderson Robertson Kerr (née Cunningham)
Father of: William, Mary, James

Vallance, Thomas, Private, 1/6th Seaforth Highlanders
Service No.: 285297
Formerly: 301767 Argyll and Sutherland Highlanders
Date Died: 17 October 1917
Aged: 32
Place of death: Passchendaele
Remembered at: Bucquoy Road Cemetery, Ficheux
Son of: John & Ann (née Gibson) Vallance, Smailholm, Roxburghshire
Sibling of: Annie, Margaret, Peter
Husband of: Euphemia (née Simpson) Vallance, High Street Earlston
Father: John, Elizabeth

Weatherston, James, Private, Royal Fusiliers
Service No.: G/67445
Date Died: 26 October 1917
Aged: 19
Place of death: Passchendaele
Remembered at: Tyne Cot Memorial
Son of: James & Margaret (née Landelles) Weatherston, 12 High Street, Earlston
Sibling of: Margaret, Mary

White, Robert Robson, Private, 1/4th Battalion King's Own Scottish Borderers
Service No.: 200758
Date Died: 19 April 1917
Aged: 24
Place of death: Second Battle of Gaza
Remembered at: Jerusalem Memorial
Son of: Isabella Robson
Sibling of: Nellie
Husband of: Isabella Hogarth Wilson

Wilkie, William, Colour Sergeant Major, 1/4th King's Own Scottish Borderers
Service No.: 4049
Date Died: 10 January 1916
Aged: 46
Place of death: At home
Remembered at: Earlston Parish Churchyard
Son of: Andrew & Jane (née Tait) Wilkie
Sibling of: Margaret, John
Husband of: Alison Hunter
Father of: Margaret

Wilson, Adam, Rifleman, London Rifle Brigade
Service No.: B/201763
Formerly: 086544 Royal Army Service Corps
Date Died: 5 April 1918
Aged: 21
Place of death: Battle of the Lys
Remembered at: Niederzwehren Cemetery, Kassel
Son of: Alexander and Margaret Wilson, Lilliesleaf, Roxburghshire
Sibling of: James, William, Catherine, Bella, Robert, Fanny

Wilson, Robert, Corporal, 3rd Traffic Control, Military Mounted Police
Service No.: P/12051
Formerly: Lothian & Border Horse, Service No. 2407
Date Died: 28 February 1919
Aged: 24
Place of death: Brandhoek
Remembered at: Cologne Southern Cemetery
Son of: Helen Hush (née Wilson)
Sibling of: Mary Jane Hush

Wilson, William, Private, 1st Battalion Scots Guards
Service No.: 12164
Date Died: 27 September 1915
Aged: 23
Place of death: Battle of Loos
Remembered at: Loos Memorial
Son of: James & Isabella Wilson, Holefield, Kelso
Sibling of: Elizabeth, Robert, Janet

Young, George, Private, 12th Highland Light Infantry
Service No.: 41840
Service No.: 8570 King's Own Scottish Borderers
Date Died: 11 April 1917
Aged: 39
Place of death: Battle of Arras
Remembered at: Arras Memorial
Son of: Archibald & Margaret Young, High Street, Earlston
Sibling of: William, Robert, Alice, Jane, Maggie, Thomas
Husband of: Agnes Kerr Young, Harden, High Street, Earlston

Young, John F., Private, 4th Battalion King's Own Scottish Borderers
Service No.: 200280
Date Died: 20 June 1918
Aged: 20
Place of death: At home
Remembered at: Earlston Parish Churchyard
Son of: William & Margaret Young, Station Road, Earlston
Sibling of: William, George, Jane, Mary

Young, Robert D., Private, 1/4th King's Own Scottish Borderers
Service No.: 6920
Date Died: 12 July 1915
Aged: 35
Place of death: Achi Baba Nullah, Gallipoli
Remembered at: Helles Memorial
Son of: Archibald & Margaret Young, High Street, Earlston
Sibling of: George, William, Thomas, Alice, Jane, Maggie
Husband of: Euphemia Young (née Scott)

Young, William Barrie, Captain, 62nd Training Squadron, Royal Air Force
Date Died: 8 August 1918
Aged: 24
Place of death: Hounslow Aerodrome
Remembered at: Earlston Parish Churchyard
Son of: Dr John & Mrs Margaret Young, The Thorne, Earlston
Sibling of: Marion, Margaret

Appendix 2

Volunteers

On Thursday, 15 October 1914, the *Southern Reporter* reported that the following men had enlisted in the military within two months of the outbreak of the war. Given the small population of Earlston, this represented approximately 40 per cent of the men eligible for military service.

Rank	Given Name	Family Name	Unit
In Army before War			
Corporal	Robert	Burns	16th Lancers
Private	George	Graham	Cameron Highlanders
Private	A.	Hood	Army Medical Corps
Private	W.	Lountain	Royal Horse Artillery
Lance Sergeant	Alex	Milne	KOSB

Rank	Given Name	Family Name	Unit
Sergeant Major	William	Milne	Royal Field Artillery
Kitchener's Army			
Private	A.	Bennett	Black Watch
Private	A.	Brockie	KOSB
Private	Alex	Cessford	KOSB
Private	Alex	Galbraith	KOSB
Private	Alex	Jack	Royal Field Artillery
Private	Alex	Whitelaw	Coldstream Guards
Private	Bert	Smith	Coldstream Guards
Private	Bertie	Smith	Lanarkshire Yeomanry
Colour Sergeant	John	Burrell	Guarding the Railways
Private	Charles	Lloyd	Motor Transport
Private	Frederick	Prince	KOSB
Private	George	Swanston	Scots Greys
Private	H.	Readman	Lothian and Border Horse
Private	Henry	Simpson	Army Service Corps

Rank	Given Name	Family Name	Unit
Private	J.	Aitchison	Cameron Highlanders
Private	J.	Robertson	Gordon Highlanders
Private	James	Calderwood	KOSB
Private	James	Dunn	5th Dragoon Guards
Private	James	Taylor	Coldstream Guards
Private	James	Thompson	Motor Transport
Private	James	Turnbull	Coldstream Guards
Private	John	McDougall	Black Watch
Private	Joseph	Perry	Border Regiment
Private	Joseph	Stirling	KOSB
Private	D.	Lountain	Guarding the Railways
Private	Matthew	Douglas	Royal Scots Fusiliers
Private	R.	Readman	Motor Transport
Private	R.D.	Young	KOSB
Private	Robert	Johnston	KOSB

Rank	Given Name	Family Name	Unit
Private	Tom	Smith	KOSB
Private	Tom D.	Smith	Scottish Rifles
Private	William	Morris	Cameron Highlanders
Private	William	Oliver	Army Service Corps
Private	William	Stirling	Cameron Highlanders
Private	William	Taylor	Army Service Corps
Private	William	Turnbull	KOSB
Private	William R.	Young	Lothian and Border Horse
Royal Navy			
Artificer	John	Donaldson	
Gunner	Adam	Girdwood	
Canadian Expeditionary Force			
	John	Baird	
	Henry	Forbes	
	James	Horseburgh	
	Alex	Maltman	
	David	Paterson	
	Stewart	Paterson	
Territorial Forces: Imperial Service			

Rank	Given Name	Family Name	Unit
Sergeant Instructor		Abbott	
Corporal	William	Aikman	
Private	James	Archibald	
Private	James	Bell	
Private	William	Betts	
Corporal	L.S.	Fisher	
Private	T.	Johnstone	
Private	A.	McLeish	
Private	J.	McLeish	
Captain	R.W.	Sharp	
Private	George	Simpson	
Home Defence			
Private	John	Aikman	
Private	G.	Aitchison	
Private	George	Aitken	
Private	D.	Ballantyne	
Private	W.	Ballantyne	
Private	G.	Brockie	
Private	James	Burns	
Private	Andrew	Burrell	
Private	George	Cessford	
Private	John	Dickson	

Rank	Given Name	Family Name	Unit
Private	Charles	Fisher	
Private	Tom	Hardie	
Private	Alexander	Kerr	
Private	Andrew	Murdison	
Private	George	Nichol	
Private	John	Reid	
Private	Andrew	Robertson	
Private	John	Robson	
Private	William	Rodger	
Private	Gavin	Rutherford	
Private	John	Simpson	
Private	William	Stafford	
Private	James	Tait	
Private	John	Thompson	
Private	Henry	Turnbull	
Colour Sergeant	William	Turnbull	
Private	William	White	
Colour Sergeant	William	Wilkie	
Private	Alex	Wilson	
Private	John	Young	

Printed in Great Britain
by Amazon